THE NEW
Art and Science
OF TEACHING

ROBERT J. MARZANO

A joint publication

 ASCD
Solution Tree

555 North Morton Street
Bloomington, IN 47404
800.733.6786 (toll free) / 812.336.7700
FAX: 812.336.7790

email: info@SolutionTree.com
SolutionTree.com

Visit **go.SolutionTree.com/instruction** to access materials related to this book.

Printed in the United States of America

Library of Congress Cataloging-in-Publication Data

Names: Marzano, Robert J., author.

Title: The new art and science of teaching / author: Robert J. Marzano.

Other titles: Art and science of teaching

Description: [Revised and expanded edition] | Bloomington, IN : Solution Tree

Press, [2017] | Includes bibliographical references and index.

Identifiers: LCCN 2016049161 | ISBN 9781943874965 (perfect bound)

Subjects: LCSH: Effective teaching--United States. | Classroom

management--United States. | Teaching--Aids and devices. | Learning,

Psychology of.

Classification: LCC LB1025.3 .M3387 2017 | DDC 371.102--dc23 LC record available at https://lccn.loc.gov/2016049161

Solution Tree
Jeffrey C. Jones, CEO
Edmund M. Ackerman, President

Solution Tree Press
President and Publisher: Douglas M. Rife
Editorial Director: Sarah Payne-Mills
Managing Production Editor: Caroline Weiss
Senior Production Editor: Suzanne Kraszewski
Senior Editor: Amy Rubenstein
Proofreader: Ashante K. Thomas
Text Designer: Laura Cox
Cover Designer: Rian Anderson
Editorial Assistants: Jessi Finn and Kendra Slayton

Table of Contents

About the Author

Robert J. Marzano, PhD, is the cofounder and chief academic officer of Marzano Resources in Denver, Colorado. During his fifty years in the field of education, he has worked with educators as a speaker and trainer and has authored more than forty books and three hundred articles on topics such as instruction, assessment, writing and implementing standards, cognition, effective leadership, and school intervention. His books include *The Art and Science of Teaching*, *Leaders of Learning*, *The Classroom Strategies Series*, *A Handbook for High Reliability Schools*, *Awaken the Learner*, and *Managing the Inner World of Teaching*. His practical translations of the most current research and theory into classroom strategies are known internationally and are widely practiced by both teachers and administrators.

He received a bachelor's degree from Iona College in New York, a master's degree from Seattle University, and a doctorate from the University of Washington.

To learn more about Robert J. Marzano's work, visit MarzanoResources.com.

To book Robert J. Marzano for professional development, contact pd@SolutionTree.com.

The History of *The New Art and Science of Teaching*

The history of *The New Art and Science of Teaching* reaches back to the 1980s when my colleagues and I synthesized the research and theory on the effective teaching of thinking in the book *Dimensions of Thinking* (Marzano et al., 1988). Relatively soon after, I authored *A Different Kind of Classroom* (Marzano, 1992), which combines strategies for teaching thinking with more general strategies for classroom management, engagement, and assessment. These works present a comprehensive synthesis of the research on teaching and provide deep-level background to *The New Art and Science of Teaching*.

The more proximal ancestry of *The New Art and Science of Teaching* dates back to the turn of the 21st century. In the book *Classroom Instruction That Works* (Marzano, Pickering, & Pollock, 2001), my colleagues and I identify nine research-supported instructional strategies. In 2003, with my colleagues I wrote a companion book titled *Classroom Management That Works* (Marzano et al., 2003) and then another companion book in 2006, *Classroom Assessment and Grading That Work* (Marzano, 2006).

While I am gratified that each book has been relatively popular and influential, I am not pleased that some have interpreted them as listings of instructional strategies that are "proven" to enhance learning for students. In fact, the nine instructional strategies in *Classroom Instruction That Works* have been commonly referred to as *high-yield instructional strategies*—a term I do not endorse. To illustrate, one need only enter the phrase "high-yield strategies" into an Internet search engine and thousands of results will be generated. In fact, in 2009, I wrote an article, "Setting the Record Straight on High-Yield Strategies" (Marzano, 2009b), to counteract the growing incorrect belief that research could ever produce a list of instructional strategies that would guarantee student learning. Specifically, I note that no single instructional strategy can guarantee student learning for a number of reasons. One is that many factors other than the use of instructional strategies affect student learning. Another is that instructional strategies work in concert or sets and should not be thought of as independent interventions. Still another is that educators have to use strategies in specific ways to produce positive results.

Over time, I created an instructional model that ties the strategies, pieces, and points together in an interactive manner; it appears in *The Art and Science of Teaching* (Marzano, 2007). I chose the phrase *art and science* purposefully to communicate a message. Specifically, research and theory will never validate the notion that teaching is simply a set of preprogrammed moves manifested as strategies. Rather, instructional strategies are best likened to techniques an artist might develop and refine over years of practice. The artist then uses these techniques to create works that are not only unique and complex but elegantly focused. The more skill the artist exhibits with available techniques, the better his or her creations. Likewise, the more skill the classroom teacher has with the instructional strategies that research and theory have uncovered over the decades, the better the teacher will be able to create lessons that optimize student learning.

The New Art and Science of Teaching, then, represents my perspective on the current state of knowledge about effective teaching. It is a perspective that certainly draws from the past but also shines light on the possible future.

The Research Supporting the Model

The research supporting *The New Art and Science of Teaching* is extensive since it covers so many years and so many previous works. I discuss the complete research history in detail in "Research Base for *The New Art and Science of Teaching*" (Marzano, 2017). I briefly summarize it here.

Narrative and Meta-Analytic Studies

The first works constituting the ancestry of *The New Art and Science of Teaching* provide narrative reviews of the literature (Marzano, 1992; Marzano et al., 1988). These reviews are quite extensive. For example, the Association for Supervision and Curriculum Development (ASCD) sponsored *Dimensions of Thinking* (Marzano et al., 1988), but a consortium of twenty-eight organizations—the Association Collaborative for Teaching Thinking—supported it. That consortium included the American Educational Research Association, the International Reading Association (now International Literacy Association), the National Council of Teachers of English, the National Council for the Social Studies, the National Science Teachers Association, and the National Council of Teachers of Mathematics, among others. In effect, *The Art and Science of Teaching* is based on some of the most widely vetted narrative reviews of the literature to that point. As the name implies, narrative reviews are author centric in that they depend on the author's ability to organize research and theory into logical categories. The author's views on the extant literature greatly influence them.

While narrative reviews were the norm at that time, the norm for research syntheses changed with the popularization of meta-analysis in the early 1990s. In *How Science Takes Stock*, Morton Hunt (1997) describes the nature and function of meta-analysis in nontechnical terms. Briefly, meta-analytic techniques translate findings into effect sizes that report how much increase or decrease in student learning can be associated with a particular intervention. Table I.1 reports the meta-analytic findings from a number of studies on the effect of goal setting as an instructional strategy.

Table I.1: Meta-Analytic Results for Goal Setting

Synthesis Study	Focus	Number of Effect Sizes (ESs)	Average ES	Percentile Gain
Wise & Okey, 1983[a]	General effects of setting goals or objectives	3 25	1.37 0.48	41 18
Chidester & Grigsby, 1984[b]	Goal difficulty	21	0.44	17
Fuchs & Fuchs, 1985[b]	Long versus short-term goals	96	0.64	24

Tubbs, 1986[c]	Goal difficulty	56	0.82	29
	Goal specificity	48	0.50	19
	Goal setting and feedback	3	0.56	21
	Participation in goal setting	17	0.002	0
Mento, Steel, & Karren, 1987[b]	Goal difficulty	118	0.58	22
Wood, Mento, & Locke, 1987[b]	Goal difficulty	72	0.58	22
	Goal specificity	53	0.43	17
Locke & Latham, 1990[c,d]	Goal difficulty	Not reported	0.52–0.82	20–29
	Goal specificity		0.42–0.80	16–29
Wright, 1990[b]	Goal difficulty	70	0.55	21
Lipsey & Wilson, 1993	General effects of setting goals or objectives	204	0.55	21
Kluger & DeNisi, 1996	Goal difficulty	37	0.51	19
Utman, 1997	Mastery versus performance goals	43	0.53	20
Donovan & Radosevich, 1998[b]	Goal commitment	21	0.36	14
Klein, Wesson, Hollenbeck, & Alge, 1999[b]	Goal commitment	83	0.47	18
Hattie, 1999[e]	Goals and feedback	121	0.46	18
Walberg, 1999	General effects of setting goals or objectives	21	0.40	16
Burns, 2004[b]	Degree of challenge	45	0.82	29
Gollwitzer & Sheeran, 2006[b]	Goal intentions on achievement	94	0.72	26
Graham & Perin, 2007	Goal specificity	5	0.70	26

[a] *Two effect sizes are listed because of the manner in which effect sizes were reported. Readers should consult that study for more details.*

[b] *As reported in Hattie (2009).*

[c] *Both Tubbs (1986) and Locke and Latham (1990) report results from organizational as well as educational settings.*

[d] *As reported in Locke and Latham (2002).*

[e] *As reported in Hattie and Timperley (2007).*

Source: Marzano, 2009a, p. 5.

Table I.1 reports eighteen synthesis studies (each row represents a synthesis study) on the topic of goal setting. The third column lists the number of effect sizes in each study. In their 1993 study, Mark Lipsey and David Wilson report 204 effect sizes; in 2007, Steve Graham and Dolores Perin report 5 effect sizes. Each effect size represents a comparison between two groups—in this case, one group that used the strategy of goal setting and one group that did not. The fourth column reports the average effect size in the synthesis study, and the fifth column reports the expected percentile gain in achievement associated with the average effect size. For example, the average effect size of 0.55 from Lipsey and Wilson (1993) is associated with an increase of 21 percentile points for an average student. The average effect size of 0.70 by Graham and Perin is associated with an increase of 26 percentile points for the average student.

Lists of meta-analytic studies like that in table I.1 appear in the following works: *A Theory-Based Meta-Analysis of Research on Instruction* (Marzano, 1998), *Classroom Instruction That Works* (Marzano et al., 2001), *Classroom Management That Works* (Marzano, 2003a), *Classroom Assessment and Grading That Work* (Marzano, 2006), *The Art and Science of Teaching* (Marzano, 2007), *Designing and Teaching Learning Goals and Objectives* (Marzano, 2009a), and *Formative Assessment and Standards-Based Grading* (Marzano, 2010b). These works as a whole include lists of effect sizes for virtually every element in *The New Art and Science of Teaching*. The studies in table I.1 include over one thousand effect sizes. If one were to list all effect sizes across these works that are foundational to *The New Art and Science of Teaching*, the final count numbers in the tens of thousands.

Teacher-Designed Studies

Since *The Art and Science of Teaching* was published in 2007, Marzano Resources (previously named Marzano Research) has conducted its own studies. Specifically, hundreds of teachers at various grade levels and in various subjects have undertaken studies of specific elements or strategies in their classrooms. In general, teachers selected a strategy they wished to study and identified content to teach to two different classes or sets of students. Instruction was the same for both groups with the exception that teachers used the selected strategy with one group of students but not the other. They used the same pretests and post-tests with both groups. Researchers then analyzed the findings and reported back to teachers.

To date, over five hundred teachers have been involved in such studies resulting in over one thousand findings reported as effect sizes. Visit **MarzanoResources.com/research/database** to access the results of each study. A series of studies summarizes many of the overall findings (see Haystead & Marzano, 2009). One of the more interesting aspects of these studies is that they were conducted with minimal and sometimes no teacher training. For the most part, teachers received either a very brief training (one half day or less) on a specific strategy, or they simply read a few pages about the strategy. This level of training probably represents the typical environment for a teacher, which involves minimal time for extensive training. The fact that the majority of teacher-designed studies demonstrated positive effect sizes in a short period of time (a few days to a few weeks) is an indicator that teachers can integrate the strategies into their repertoire of techniques relatively quickly.

Schoolwide Studies

Schoolwide studies examine the effects of *The Art and Science of Teaching* model on the average achievement scores for the school as a whole as opposed to the average achievement scores of students in the classes of specific teachers. For example, one study involves fifty-nine schools and 1,117 teachers. It examines the relationship between teachers' usage of instructional strategies and the school's average score on state tests of mathematics and reading (see Marzano Resources, 2010, 2011). Effect sizes ranged from 0.53 in mathematics to 0.74 in reading.

Teacher Evaluation Studies

The Art and Science of Teaching as a teacher evaluation model is used in eleven countries, three provinces in Canada, and forty-three states (Basileo & Marzano, 2016). Data from these implementations indicate a relationship between teachers' use of the strategies in the model and growth in student learning. Growth is commonly determined by value-added measures that are based on state tests at the end of the year. The book

Teacher Evaluation That Makes a Difference (Marzano & Toth, 2013) discuses value-added measures in depth. Briefly though, the strength of value-added measures is that they compute student learning over a given year while controlling for students' previous learning and demographics. These studies demonstrate that teachers' scores on the model as a whole are positively and significantly correlated with value-added measures based on state tests (see Basileo, Toth, & Kennedy, 2015). Perhaps more important, the studies demonstrate that the individual elements in the model are positively and significantly correlated with value-added measures (see Basileo & Marzano, 2016). Most noteworthy about these studies is that they involve over one hundred and eighty thousand teacher observations spread over three school years (2012 to 2015).

The Major Features of *The New Art and Science of Teaching*

The New Art and Science of Teaching is new, even though the original strategies are intact, albeit greatly expanded. One of the major changes in *The New Art and Science of Teaching* is that it takes a student-outcomes perspective as opposed to a teacher-outcomes perspective. To illustrate, *The Art and Science of Teaching* identifies specific teacher behaviors. Teachers can use rating scales for each element of the model to determine the extent to which they are effectively deploying instructional strategies. While this is useful information, *The New Art and Science of Teaching* has a focus on student outcomes. This makes intuitive sense since instructional strategies generate certain mental states and processes in learners' minds which, in turn, enhance students' learning. Figure I.1 illustrates the teaching and learning progression.

Figure I.1: The teaching and learning progression.

According to figure I.1, specific mental states and processes in learners' minds are the mediating variable between the effective application of instructional strategies and enhanced student learning. Without these mental states and processes, a given strategy will have little or no effect on students. As subsequent chapters in this book illustrate, this single fact changes the way districts, schools, and classroom educators should monitor the use of instructional strategies, provide teachers with feedback, and analyze students' learning. Table I.2 depicts the specific mental states and processes that should be present in the learner's mind.

Table I.2: Teacher Actions and Student Mental States and Processes

	Teacher Actions	**Student Mental States and Processes**
Feedback	Providing and Communicating Clear Learning Goals	1. Students understand the progression of knowledge they are expected to master and where they are along that progression.
	Using Assessments	2. Students understand how test scores and grades relate to their status on the progression of knowledge they are expected to master.

continued →

	Teacher Actions	Student Mental States and Processes
Content	Conducting Direct Instruction Lessons	3. When content is new, students understand which parts are important and how the parts fit together.
	Conducting Practicing and Deepening Lessons	4. After teachers present new content, students deepen their understanding and develop fluency in skills and processes.
	Conducting Knowledge Application Lessons	5. After teachers present new content, students generate and defend claims through knowledge application tasks.
	Using Strategies That Appear in All Types of Lessons	6. Students continually integrate new knowledge with old knowledge and revise their understanding accordingly.
Context	Using Engagement Strategies	7. Students are paying attention, energized, intrigued, and inspired.
	Implementing Rules and Procedures	8. Students understand and follow rules and procedures.
	Building Relationships	9. Students feel welcome, accepted, and valued.
	Communicating High Expectations	10. Typically reluctant students feel valued and do not hesitate to interact with the teacher or their peers.

The mental states and processes in table I.2 are organized in three major categories: (1) feedback, (2) content, and (3) context. *Feedback* refers to the information loop between the teacher and the students that provides students with an awareness of what they should be learning and how they are doing. *Content* refers to lesson progression, which allows students to move from an initial understanding of content to application of content while continuously reviewing and upgrading their knowledge. *Context* refers to the following student psychological needs: engagement, order, a sense of belonging, and high expectations.

The column Teacher Actions corresponds to each desired mental state and process. For example, the desired mental state of students understanding the progression of knowledge they are expected to master and where they are along that progression (the first row in table I.2) is associated with the teacher action of providing and communicating clear learning goals. Students' understanding which parts of newly presented content are important and how the parts fit together (the third row) is associated with the teacher action of conducting direct instruction lessons. Students paying attention, being energized, being intrigued, and being inspired (the seventh row) is associated with the teacher's use of engagement strategies, and so on.

The teacher actions and student mental states and processes translate nicely into a set of questions that help teachers plan units and lessons within those units. In *The New Art and Science of Teaching*, these are referred to as *design questions*. Table I.3 depicts these.

Table I.3: Design Questions

	Design Areas	Design Questions
Feedback	1. Providing and Communicating Clear Learning Goals	How will I communicate clear learning goals that help students understand the progression of knowledge they are expected to master and where they are along that progression?
	2. Using Assessments	How will I design and administer assessments that help students understand how their test scores and grades are related to their status on the progression of knowledge they are expected to master?

Content	3. Conducting Direct Instruction Lessons	When content is new, how will I design and deliver direct instruction lessons that help students understand which parts are important and how the parts fit together?
	4. Conducting Practicing and Deepening Lessons	After presenting content, how will I design and deliver lessons that help students deepen their understanding and develop fluency in skills and processes?
	5. Conducting Knowledge Application Lessons	After presenting content, how will I design and deliver lessons that help students generate and defend claims through knowledge application?
	6. Using Strategies That Appear in All Types of Lessons	Throughout all types of lessons, what strategies will I use to help students continually integrate new knowledge with old knowledge and revise their understanding accordingly?
Context	7. Using Engagement Strategies	What engagement strategies will I use to help students pay attention, be energized, be intrigued, and be inspired?
	8. Implementing Rules and Procedures	What strategies will I use to help students understand and follow rules and procedures?
	9. Building Relationships	What strategies will I use to help students feel welcome, accepted, and valued?
	10. Communicating High Expectations	What strategies will I use to help typically reluctant students feel valued and comfortable interacting with me and their peers?

These ten design questions and the general framework with the three categories provide a road map for lesson and unit planning that not only points to specific strategies but also ensures a focus on student outcomes. Additionally, the framework helps organize a wide array of instructional strategies into a comprehensive network. To illustrate, consider table I.4 (page 8).

Table I.4 depicts forty-three categories of instructional strategies (referred to as *elements*) embedded in the ten design areas found within three general categories. These forty-three elements address instructional strategies detailed in the multiple and diverse sources briefly mentioned at the beginning of this introduction (Marzano, 1992, 2006, 2007, 2010; Marzano et al., 1988; Marzano et al., 2001; Marzano et al., 2003). Additionally, each element involves multiple strategies. For example, consider element twenty-four within the design area of engagement: increasing response rates. It includes the following nine strategies—nine different ways to increase students' response rates.

1. Random names
2. Hand signals
3. Response cards
4. Response chaining
5. Paired response
6. Choral response
7. Wait time
8. Elaborative interrogation
9. Multiple types of questions

In all, *The New Art and Science of Teaching* involves over 330 specific instructional strategies embedded in the forty-three elements.

Table I.4: Elements Within the Ten Design Areas

Feedback	Content	Context
Providing and Communicating Clear Learning Goals 1. Providing scales and rubrics 2. Tracking student progress 3. Celebrating success **Using Assessments** 4. Using informal assessments of the whole class 5. Using formal assessments of individual students	**Conducting Direct Instruction Lessons** 6. Chunking content 7. Processing content 8. Recording and representing content **Conducting Practicing and Deepening Lessons** 9. Using structured practice sessions 10. Examining similarities and differences 11. Examining errors in reasoning **Conducting Knowledge Application Lessons** 12. Engaging students in cognitively complex tasks 13. Providing resources and guidance 14. Generating and defending claims **Using Strategies That Appear in All Types of Lessons** 15. Previewing strategies 16. Highlighting critical information 17. Reviewing content 18. Revising knowledge 19. Reflecting on learning 20. Assigning purposeful homework 21. Elaborating on information 22. Organizing students to interact	**Using Engagement Strategies** 23. Noticing and reacting when students are not engaged 24. Increasing response rates 25. Using physical movement 26. Maintaining a lively pace 27. Demonstrating intensity and enthusiasm 28. Presenting unusual information 29. Using friendly controversy 30. Using academic games 31. Providing opportunities for students to talk about themselves 32. Motivating and inspiring students **Implementing Rules and Procedures** 33. Establishing rules and procedures 34. Organizing the physical layout of the classroom 35. Demonstrating withitness 36. Acknowledging adherence to rules and procedures 37. Acknowledging lack of adherence to rules and procedures **Building Relationships** 38. Using verbal and nonverbal behaviors that indicate affection for students 39. Understanding students' backgrounds and interests 40. Displaying objectivity and control **Communicating High Expectations** 41. Demonstrating value and respect for reluctant learners 42. Asking in-depth questions of reluctant learners 43. Probing incorrect answers with reluctant learners

The Old and New Art and Science of Teaching

The New Art and Science of Teaching has many similarities with the initial framework, although it has undergone significant changes. For example, both the original and revised framework have three overarching categories. The original three overarching lesson categories are (1) routine segments, (2) content segments, and (3) on-the-spot segments. As their names imply, classrooms engage in *routine segments* on a systematic basis, *content segments* address content lessons, and *on-the-spot segments* address strategies that teachers use when unplanned, immediate situations occur. Again, these three categories emanate from the perspective of what the teacher does. The three overarching categories in *The New Art and Science of Teaching* emanate from a perspective of what must occur in students' minds to learn effectively. Specifically, (1) they must receive feedback, (2) they must receive content instruction that triggers specific types of thinking, and (3) they must have a psychological context in which their basic needs are met.

The Art and Science of Teaching has design questions, as does *The New Art and Science of Teaching*. Indeed, eight of the design questions in *The New Art and Science of Teaching* are basically identical to the originals. However, *The New Art and Science of Teaching* has two design questions that are not part of the original: one deals with assessment (design question 2: How will I design and administer assessments that help students understand how their test scores and grades are related to their status on the progression of knowledge they are expected to master?); the other deals with the continuous development of understanding (design question 6: Throughout all types of lessons, what strategies will I use to help students continually integrate new knowledge with old knowledge and revise their understanding accordingly?).

Both versions of *The Art and Science of Teaching* have categories of instructional strategies referred to as *elements*. The original version has forty-one elements; the new version has forty-three. Of the forty-three elements in the new model, thirty-nine are identical to the old model. Thus, four elements in the new model are not in the old. (For a detailed comparison of elements from the old and new models, visit **go.SolutionTree.com/instruction** to view the Compendium Crosswalk.)

Finally, both *The Art and Science of Teaching* and *The New Art and Science of Teaching* identify specific instructional strategies for each element. As mentioned previously, *The New Art and Science of Teaching* has more strategies than the original version. Specifically, the book *Becoming a Reflective Teacher* (Marzano, 2012), which is based on the original model, identifies 280 strategies. *The New Art and Science of Teaching* identifies over 330 specific strategies.

A Framework for Change

The New Art and Science of Teaching, however, is much more than an update of the original model. Rather, it is a framework for substantive change. Indeed, one might even consider it a manifesto.

At its core, a manifesto is a written statement that describes a person's or group's policies and goals. *The New Art and Science of Teaching* describes those changes at the individual teacher level, school level, and district level that I believe are warranted by the research in education since the 1960s and through my observations of teachers, schools, and districts during that time. As such, each chapter includes a section titled Implications for Change that describes how the model elements highlight alterations teachers must make in current practice. Additionally, each chapter contains a section on planning issues teachers should consider.

Chapters 1 and 2 address the elements in the overall category of feedback. Chapter 1 examines providing and communicating clear learning goals, and chapter 2 considers assessment.

Chapters 3 through 6 address the overall category of content. Chapter 3 considers direct instruction lessons. Chapter 4 examines practicing and deepening lessons. Chapter 5 addresses implementing knowledge application lessons. Chapter 6 presents strategies that teachers should use in all three types of lessons.

Chapters 7 through 10 address the overall category of context. Chapter 7 focuses on engagement. Chapter 8 examines implementing rules and procedures. Chapter 9 spotlights strategies for building relationships, and chapter 10 focuses on communicating high expectations with an emphasis on the reluctant learner.

The final chapter of this book addresses change at the macro level. Specifically, it addresses eight recommended system-level changes that are logical consequences of *The New Art and Science of Teaching* framework.

CHAPTER 1

Providing and Communicating Clear Learning Goals

Effective feedback begins with clearly defined and clearly communicated learning goals.

> The desired mental states and processes
> for clear learning goals are that:
>
> Students understand the progression of
> knowledge they are expected to master and where
> they are along that progression.

The importance of achieving these mental states and processes in students is almost self-evident. If students understand what they are to learn during a given lesson or unit, they are better able to determine how well they are doing and what they need to improve.

Note that this design area addresses concepts for which there are many misconceptions and diverse perspectives. Specifically, terms like *proficiency scale*, *rubric*, *learning goal*, *learning objective*, *learning target*, *behavioral objective*, and the like have different meanings. For a historical perspective on these terms, see Marzano and John S. Kendall (2007, 2008). I recommend that districts and schools operationally define these terms for themselves. As long as schools use the terms in an internally consistent manner, they will be on sound footing.

The following elements are important to providing clear goals.

Element 1: Providing Scales and Rubrics

Scales and rubrics are necessary if students are to understand the progression of knowledge they are expected to learn. The terms *scales* and *rubrics* are frequently interchangeable, but there are important distinctions. Rubrics tend to be specific to one task. For example, a teacher might design a rubric to examine student performance on a specific writing prompt like "Describe your favorite animal and what makes the animal special." A scale is more general and describes a progression of knowledge or skill. For example, a scale might describe the progression of knowledge leading up to a clear understanding of the concept of buoyancy or the progression of knowledge leading up to an ability to convert fractions into decimals. Although rubrics have their place in the classroom, *The New Art and Science of Teaching* focuses on the use of proficiency scales, especially for academic content. Figure 1.1 (page 12) provides a sample scale.

4.0	The student will prove the claims in an argument by providing relevant and sufficient evidence and by acknowledging and refuting a counterclaim (for example, develop a claim about the importance of free speech, find evidence that supports the claim and a counterclaim, and construct an argument that validates the claim and refutes the counterclaim).
3.5	In addition to score 3.0 performance, the student has partial success at score 4.0 content.
3.0	The student will: • 3.1—Generate claims and distinguish them from counterclaims (for example, generate a claim about the use of cellphones as educational tools in schools, generate a counterclaim that argues the opposite position, and describe why a person might take either position). • 3.2—Support claims with relevant and sufficient evidence as well as logical reasoning (for example, use evidence from the text to support a claim about the purpose for Walt Whitman's contrasting tones in "O Captain! My Captain!").
2.5	The student has no major errors or omissions regarding score 2.0 content, and partial success at score 3.0 content.
2.0	The student will: • 2.1—Recognize or recall specific vocabulary (for example, *backing*, *claim*, *counterclaim*, *grounds*, and *qualifier*) and perform basic processes such as the following. ♦ Describe the qualities of a claim (for example, it should be specific and should be an opinion that can be proved using evidence) ♦ Describe the roles of grounds, backing, and qualifiers in a claim ♦ Make a general claim more specific by incorporating details ♦ Compare two opposing claims for the same argument • 2.2—Recognize or recall specific vocabulary (for example, *logical*, *reasoning*, *relevant*, and *sufficient*) and perform basic processes such as: ♦ Describe different types of evidence that can support a claim ♦ Annotate notes and texts for evidence that could support a claim ♦ Explain why it is important to have relevant and sufficient evidence ♦ Explain how a piece of evidence supports a claim
1.5	The student has partial success at score 2.0 content, and major errors or omissions regarding score 3.0 content.
1.0	With help, the student has partial success at score 2.0 content and score 3.0 content.
0.5	With help, the student has partial success at score 2.0 content but not at score 3.0 content.
0.0	Even with help, the student has no success.

Figure 1.1: Sample scale for generating claims, evidence, and reasoning at grade 8.

Figure 1.1 is a scale for the topic of generating claims, evidence, and reasoning at grade 8. While there are many ways to create scales and rubrics, I recommend the format in figure 1.1. It has five levels of proficiency, ranging from 0.0 to 4.0 with half-point scores. However, there are only three levels of explicit content at scores 2.0, 3.0, and 4.0. Score 3.0 is the desired level of proficiency students are to meet. Score 2.0 content is that which is foundational to score 3.0 content and is directly taught. Score 4.0 involves inferences and applications that go beyond score 3.0 content. Score 1.0 indicates partial success with help; score 0.0 indicates no success even with help. The half-point scores show the partial success necessary to achieve each score. (For a detailed discussion of proficiency scales, see Marzano, 2006, 2009a, 2010b.)

There are a variety of specific strategies that make the use of scales effective and efficient. These appear in table 1.1 along with brief descriptions.

Table 1.1: Strategies for Providing Scales and Rubrics

Strategy	Description
Clearly articulating learning goals	The teacher clarifies learning goals that state what students will know or be able to do at the end of a unit or set of lessons.
Creating scales or rubrics for learning goals	Learning goals are much more useful when embedded in a proficiency scale (also referred to as a performance scale). Teachers do this by articulating a learning target for score 3.0, a simpler learning goal for score 2.0, and a more complex learning goal for score 4.0.
Implementing routines for using targets and scales	The teacher uses routines to encourage students' attentiveness to learning targets and proficiency scales. A routine could be as simple as reviewing a scale or learning target at the beginning of each class, or it could be more complex and require students to explain components of the target or scale.
Using teacher-created targets and scales	After designing scales with embedded learning targets, the teacher uses them as the basis for instruction. For example, at the beginning of the set of lessons focused on a particular scale, the teacher might spend a class period or two on each of the score 2.0 targets.
Creating student-friendly scales	The teacher asks students to translate scales into student-friendly language. After the teacher explains the target, as well as the simpler and more complex learning goals to students, students work in small groups to create their own wording for the 2.0, 3.0, and 4.0 learning goals.
Identifying individual student learning goals	The teacher asks students to identify a personal learning goal that interests them and that relates to the teacher-identified learning goals. Students record their personal learning goals.

Source: Adapted from Marzano Resources, 2016ee.

Some of the strategies in table 1.1 focus on the creation of proficiency scales. For example, the strategy clearly articulating learning goals deals with the internal structure of a proficiency scale. In essence, a proficiency scale is a continuum of learning goals (also referred to as *learning targets*).

Other strategies deal with the use of proficiency scales for instructional purposes. For example, consider the strategy implementing routines for using targets and scales. One routine is to refer to learning goals on a daily basis and describe where the learning goals fit within the proficiency scale. A teacher might have the proficiency scale for a particular unit posted on the wall. Before she begins a lesson, she refers back to the scale and points to the precise element of the scale on which the current lesson will focus. She refers to the element of focus as "today's learning target." She then asks students to restate the learning target as an "I can" statement.

Some of the strategies deal with making proficiency scales more understandable to students. For example, the strategy creating student-friendly scales involves translating a scale into student-friendly language by having groups of students or the class as a whole rewrite score 2.0, score 3.0, and score 4.0 descriptors.

When the strategies in this element produce the desired effects, teachers will observe the following behaviors in students.

- Students can explain the proficiency scale in their own words.
- Students can explain what learning goal is being addressed in the current lesson.
- Students can describe how the current activity relates to the target goal.
- Students can explain the progression of content on the scale.

Element 2: Tracking Student Progress

With proficiency scales in place, the teacher can help provide each student with a clear sense of where he or she started relative to a topic and where he or she is currently. This is one of the most powerful uses of a proficiency scale because it allows students to see their growth along a continuum of knowledge. To illustrate, consider figure 1.2.

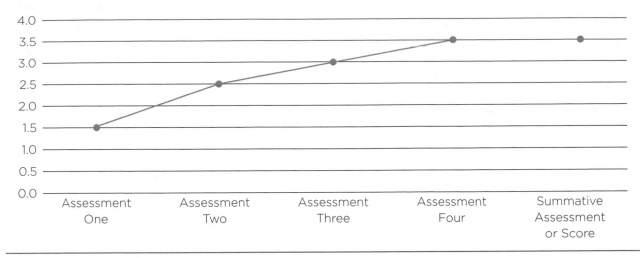

Figure 1.2: Student growth across five assessments on the same topic.

Figure 1.2 depicts an individual student's progress on one topic for which there is a proficiency scale. The student began with a score of 1.5 but rose to a score of 3.5 over five assessments. Observing their growth on a topic is intrinsically motivating to students simply because people react positively to evidence that they are progressing (Hattie & Timperley, 2007).

Table 1.2 lists a number of strategies and activities that relate to element 2.

Table 1.2: Tracking Student Progress

Strategy	Description
Using formative scores	Using formative scores throughout a unit of instruction helps teachers and students monitor progress and adjust if necessary. This is different from summative scores, which represent a student's status at the end of a particular point in time.
Designing assessments that generate formative scores	To design assessments that generate formative scores for a particular proficiency scale, a teacher develops items or tasks that correspond directly to content in levels 2.0, 3.0, and 4.0 of the scale.
Using individual score-level assessments	The teacher uses assessments that evaluate only one level of a scale (for example, only 2.0 content) to measure students' knowledge or to allow students to progress at their own pace through the levels of a scale.
Using different types of assessments	To collect formative scores over time that pertain to a specific proficiency scale, the teacher uses obtrusive assessments (which interrupt the flow of classroom activity), unobtrusive assessments (which do not interrupt classroom activities), or student-generated assessments.

Generating summative scores	The teacher makes use of several different approaches to generating summative scores for a specific proficiency scale. Approaches range from using formative scores to assign a summative score to designing a specific assessment to assign a summative score. Where formative scores track students' progress over time, a summative score indicates an individual student's status at the end of a specific interval of time such as a grading period.
Charting student progress	The student sets a goal relative to a specific scale at the beginning of a unit or grading period and then tracks his or her scores on that scale. At the end of the unit or grading period, the teacher assigns a final, or summative, score to the student for the scale.
Charting class progress	The teacher tracks the entire class' progress by showing what percentage of students scored at a proficient (3.0) level or above for a particular assessment.

Source: Adapted from Marzano Resources, 2016ll.

Some of the strategies in table 1.2 involve making a distinction between the various uses of scores generated from a proficiency scale. To illustrate, consider the strategy using formative scores and the strategy generating summative scores. When using proficiency scales, these terms take on a clear meaning. Specifically, the time the teacher administers an assessment, as opposed to the assessment's format, determines whether its score is formative or summative. To illustrate, reconsider figure 1.2. The first four scores in the figure are formative. They provide evidence to compute the final score—the summative score. In effect, a teacher can assign a summative score without actually using a specific summative assessment. (For a detailed discussion, see Marzano, 2006, 2010b.)

Some strategies expand the scope of what defines an assessment. Consider the strategy using different types of assessments. It describes three general types of assessments: (1) obtrusive assessments, (2) unobtrusive assessments, and (3) student-generated assessments. As their name implies, *obtrusive assessments* interrupt the flow of instruction. Teaching stops; assessment occurs. Typically, obtrusive assessments are pencil and paper in nature. Classroom teachers tend to use obtrusive assessments almost exclusively. *Unobtrusive assessments* do not interrupt the flow of instruction and commonly take the form of observations while students are working. *Student-generated assessments* are the most unique and potentially powerful form of assessment because students determine how they might demonstrate proficiency on a particular topic. Student-generated assessments help develop student agency because they give some decision-making power to those who are being assessed.

When the strategies in this element produce the desired effects, teachers will observe the following behaviors in students.

- Students can describe how they have progressed on a particular proficiency scale.
- Students periodically update their status on a proficiency scale.
- Students can describe what they need to do to get to the next level of performance.

Element 3: Celebrating Success

Providing scales (element 1) and tracking students' progress (element 2) on those scales allow for the celebration of two types of success: status and growth. *Status* refers to a student's score at a particular moment in time. *Growth* refers to the difference between the student's current and first scores on the topic. A student grows when his or her scores on a scale rise over time.

Table 1.3 (page 16) lists the strategies for this element.

Table 1.3: Celebrating Success

Strategy	Description
Status celebration	The teacher celebrates each student's status at any point in time, including at the end of a unit.
Knowledge gain celebration	The teacher celebrates knowledge gain, which is the difference between a student's initial and final scores for a learning goal. To do this, the teacher recognizes the growth each student has made over the course of a unit.
Verbal feedback	The teacher emphasizes each student's effort and growth by specifically explaining what a student did well on a task.

Source: Adapted from Marzano Resources, 2016d.

The first two strategies in table 1.3 address formal ways of acknowledging students' status and growth. The teacher might have celebrations, such as by ringing a bell, each time a student reaches score 3.0 on a proficiency scale. At the end of a unit, the teacher might also acknowledge all students who have increased their original score by 1.5 or more scale points. Students might simply stand and receive a round of applause from their classmates. Verbal feedback might involve private or public comments to students. The structure of a proficiency scale allows for multiple celebrations of both status and growth.

When the strategies in this element produce the desired effects, teachers will observe the following behaviors in students.

- Students demonstrate pride regarding their accomplishments in class.
- Students appear to strive for higher scores on a proficiency scale.
- Students say they enjoy celebrations.

Planning

The design question pertaining to providing and communicating clear goals and objectives is, How will I communicate clear learning goals that help students understand the progression of knowledge they are expected to master and where they are along that progression? The three elements that pertain to this design area provide specific guidance regarding this overall design question. Teachers can easily turn these elements into more focused planning questions.

- **Element 1:** How will I design scales or rubrics?
- **Element 2:** How will I track progress?
- **Element 3:** How will I celebrate success?

For a given unit, a teacher should think carefully about the content and select what is essential. This is not an easy task in an era of standards. It is a common practice for teachers to plan their instruction around a specific standard. For example, a fourth-grade science teacher might plan a unit of instruction around the following science standard:

> Make observations and/or measurements to provide evidence of the effects of weathering or the rate of erosion by water, ice, wind, or vegetation. (Achieve, 2013, p. 35)

This single standard has a wide array of embedded content. In fact, the following content is implicit in this single standard (Marzano & Simms, 2014).

- Students will be able to make observations.
- Students will be able to make measurements.

- Students will understand what evidence is and be able to provide evidence.
- Students will understand what weathering is and will be able to recognize the effects of weathering.
- Students will understand what erosion is and be able to recognize erosion.
- Students will understand how water, ice, and wind affect erosion.
- Students will understand how vegetation affects erosion. (p. 108)

The teacher's first tasks relative to this design area are to unpack the standard, identify what is essential, and organize the content into a proficiency scale. Such a scale for this standard appears in figure 1.3.

4.0	The student will research a solution that addresses a cause of weathering and erosion (for example, investigate the rate of erosion by a local stream, determine how human activity impacts this rate, and implement a solution that reduces the effect of human activity, such as planting vegetation by the stream bank or maintaining a designated trail through the area).
3.5	In addition to score 3.0 performance, the student has partial success at score 4.0 content.
3.0	The student will identify factors that contribute to weathering and erosion (for example, explain how weathering and erosion are caused by water, ice, wind, and vegetation, and identify factors that increase the effect and rate of weathering and erosion).
2.5	The student has no major errors or omissions regarding score 2.0 content, and partial success at score 3.0 content.
2.0	The student will recognize or recall specific vocabulary (for example, *erosion*, *sediment*, *water*, *weathering*, and *wind*) and perform basic processes such as: <ul><li>Explain the difference between weathering and erosion (weathering breaks down rocks and minerals into smaller pieces, while erosion moves the smaller pieces from place to place).</li><li>Identify causes of weathering (for example, precipitation, ice, wind, acid rain, water, and vegetation).</li><li>Identify causes of erosion (for example, wind, water, gravity, snow, and ice).</li><li>Compare the effects of weathering and erosion over time (for example, a river may not seem to be causing erosion when observed daily but can carve out canyons over long spans of time).</li><li>Explain how erosion causes deposition of weathered sediments.</li></ul>
1.5	The student has partial success at score 2.0 content, and major errors or omissions regarding score 3.0 content.
1.0	With help, the student has partial success at score 2.0 content and score 3.0 content.
0.5	With help, the student has partial success at score 2.0 content but not at score 3.0 content.
0.0	Even with help, the student has no success.

Figure 1.3: Scale for weathering and erosion at grade 4.

With the scale in place, the stage is set for students to track their progress. As figure 1.2 (page 14) shows, the student began with a score of 1.5, indicating partial success at score 2.0. By the end of the unit, the student achieved a score of 3.5, indicating success at score 2.0 and 3.0 content and partial success with score 4.0 content. The student gained two full points on the proficiency scale.

Implications for Change

The New Art and Science of Teaching is a framework for change. Indeed, each of the ten design areas has implications for substantive change. The change that providing and communicating clear learning goals and objectives implies is the manner in which educators view content. The prevailing view is that classroom content directly equates with standards. A teacher receives standards from the state or district. These standards represent the content to teach. Unfortunately, such a process is almost impossible to execute. A historical perspective provides evidence for this assertion.

The modern standards movement began in 1989 at the first Education Summit in Charlottesville, Virginia, and has continued to evolve. (For a discussion, see Marzano & Kendall, 1996.) Every state now has its own set of standards, which the Common Core State Standards (CCSS) for English language arts (National Governors Association Center for Best Practices & Council of Chief State School Officers [NGA & CCSSO], 2010a) and mathematics (NGA & CCSSO, 2010b) and the Next Generation Science Standards (NGSS Lead States, 2013) influence to some degree small or large.

After decades of evolution, one might think that standards in every subject area have been fine-tuned to a high degree of precision and focus. However, this is not the case. To illustrate, at the beginning of the 21st century, researchers estimated that it would take about 15,500 hours to teach all the standards identified for K–12 students, yet there were only about 9,000 hours of instructional time available to do so (see Marzano, 2007; Marzano & Kendall, 1996). In effect, it was impossible to teach the content in the standards in the time available.

The trend in the disparity between the amount of content the standards addressed and the time available to teach it persists. For example, Marzano, David C. Yanoski, Jan K. Hoegh, and Simms (2013) identify seventy-three standards statements for eighth-grade English language arts in the CCSS. As shown in the previous section, each of these standards contains a number of unique topics. Assuming an average of five topics per standards statement, there are 365 English language arts topics eighth-grade teachers are expected to address; obviously this is an impossible task within the confines of a 180-day school year.

Proficiency scales provide a solution to this problem. Individual teachers could take the initiative to unpack the standards they addressed in a unit and create one or more proficiency scales that focus on the important content. However, such a task is better addressed at the district level. That is, district curriculum experts working with teachers should create proficiency scales for each subject area at each grade level. Tammy Heflebower, Hoegh, and Phil Warrick (2014) articulate specific steps as to how a district might do this. Additionally, at Marzano Research (since renamed Marzano Resources), Julia Simms (2016) led a team identifying the essential topics (referred to as *measurement topics*) for English language arts, mathematics, and science. Figure 1.4 lists the topics for eighth-grade English language arts.

Measurement	Topics
Analyzing text organization and structure	Generating claims, evidence, and reasoning
Analyzing ideas and themes	Generating narratives
Analyzing claims, evidence, and reasoning	Finding sources and research
Analyzing narratives	Determining audience purpose and task
Analyzing point of view and purpose	Revising
Comparing texts	Using parts of speech
Analyzing language	Editing
Generating text organization and structure	

Source: Adapted from Simms, 2016.

Figure 1.4: Eighth-grade English language arts topics.

For each measurement topic, the team developed proficiency scales that districts and schools can customize by adding, altering, or deleting the text. To illustrate, figure 1.5 reports the proficiency scale for the topic of generating claims, evidence, and reasoning (GCER).

4.0	The student will prove the claims in an argument by providing relevant and sufficient evidence and by acknowledging and refuting a counterclaim (for example, develop a claim about the importance of free speech, find evidence that supports the claim and a counterclaim, and construct an argument that validates the claim and refutes the counterclaim).
3.5	In addition to score 3.0 performance, the student has partial success at score 4.0 content.
3.0	The student will: • GCER1—Generate claims and distinguish them from counterclaims (for example, generate a claim about the use of cellphones as educational tools in schools, generate a counterclaim that argues the opposite position, and describe why a person might take either position). • GCER2—Support claims with relevant and sufficient evidence as well as logical reasoning (for example, use evidence from the text to support a claim about the purpose for Walt Whitman's contrasting tones in "O Captain! My Captain!").
2.5	The student has no major errors or omissions regarding score 2.0 content, and partial success at score 3.0 content.

2.0	The student will:
	
	• GCER1—Recognize or recall specific vocabulary (for example, *backing*, *claim*, *counterclaim*, *evidence*, *fact*, *general*, *grounds*, *opinion*, *prompt*, *qualifier*, and *specific*) and perform basic processes such as the following.
	
	  ♦ Describe the qualities of a claim (for example, it should be specific and should be an opinion that can be proved using evidence).
	
	  ♦ Describe the roles of grounds, backing, and qualifiers in a claim.
	
	  ♦ Describe two possible arguments a person could make about a particular topic.
	
	  ♦ Explain the grounds for two contrasting claims.
	
	  ♦ Make a general claim more specific by incorporating details.
	
	  ♦ Make a specific claim more general by removing details.
	
	  ♦ Compare two opposing claims for the same argument.
	
	• GCER2—Recognize or recall specific vocabulary (for example, *claim*, *evidence*, *logical*, *reasoning*, *relevant*, and *sufficient*) and perform basic processes such as the following.
	
	  ♦ Describe different types of evidence that can support a claim.
	
	  ♦ Annotate notes and texts for evidence that could support a claim.
	
	  ♦ Find specific pieces of evidence and add them to an outline.
	
	  ♦ Explain why it is important to have relevant and sufficient evidence.
	
	  ♦ Annotate a paragraph's claims and matching evidence in coordinating colors.
	
	  ♦ Explain how a piece of evidence supports a claim.
	
	  ♦ Use evidence to determine the backing and qualifier for a claim.

1.5	The student has partial success at score 2.0 content, and major errors or omissions regarding score 3.0 content.
1.0	With help, the student has partial success at score 2.0 content and score 3.0 content.
0.5	With help, the student has partial success at score 2.0 content but not at score 3.0 content.
0.0	Even with help, the student has no success.

Figure 1.5: Critical concepts scale for generating claims, evidence, and reasoning at grade 8.

In all, about five-hundred proficiency scales like the one in figure 1.5 have been written for mathematics, English language arts, and science for grades K–12. This is a number that teachers could address in the time available. If district personnel wish to create their own, they should unpack their state standards and identify a small set of topics (fifteen to twenty-five) to focus on during instruction and assessment at each grade level for each content area. This rather straightforward effort solves a problem I believe is one of the most serious plaguing K–12 education: namely, a curriculum that is so bloated and cumbersome that it is impossible for teachers to teach well and, therefore, difficult for students to learn efficiently.

CHAPTER 2

Using Assessments

At its core, assessment is a feedback mechanism for students and teachers. Assessments should provide students with information about how to advance their understanding of content and teachers with information about how to help students do so.

> The desired mental states and processes for assessment are that:
>
> Students understand how test scores
> and grades relate to their status on the progression
> of knowledge they are expected to master.

To achieve these outcomes in students, there must be a transparent relationship between students' scores on assessments and their progress on a proficiency scale. The following elements are important to effective assessment.

Element 4: Using Informal Assessments of the Whole Class

Informal assessments of the whole class provide a barometer of how the whole class is performing regarding the progression of knowledge articulated in a specific proficiency scale. Informal whole-class assessments typically don't involve individual students' recorded scores. The specific strategies associated with this element appear in table 2.1 (page 22).

The strategies in table 2.1 provide teachers with a wide array of options for informal assessment. Teachers can execute voting techniques quickly and repeat them multiple times. For example, the teacher asks a series of multiple-choice questions on score 2.0 content from a proficiency scale using PowerPoint slides. Students then use voting devices (such as clickers) to signify their answers. The teacher keeps track of the number of students who vote on the correct answers but does not record individual student scores. However, the teacher does report on the percentage of students with correct answers and uses that percentage as a barometer of how well the class as a whole is doing on score 2.0 content.

Response boards are similar to voting techniques. However, they provide more information. With this technique, students record their responses on erasable boards that are small enough for them to handle individually. Response boards allow for students to write short constructed-response answers. Upon the teacher's

Table 2.1: Using Informal Assessments of the Whole Class

Strategy	Description
Confidence rating techniques	The teacher asks students to rate how confident they are in their understanding of a topic using hand signals (thumbs-up, thumbs-sideways, or thumbs-down) or using technology (for example, clickers or cell phones).
Voting techniques	The teacher asks students to vote on answers to specific questions or prompts.
Response boards	The teacher asks students to write their responses to a question or prompt on an erasable response board or response card.
Unrecorded assessments	The teacher administers an assessment and immediately has students score their own tests. The teacher uses scores as feedback but does not record them.

Source: Adapted from Marzano Resources, 2016s.

direction, students hold their response boards up so only the teacher can see. The teacher quickly surveys student responses and reports on what percentage of the class seems to know the correct answer.

When the strategies in this element produce the desired effects, teachers will observe the following behaviors in students.

- Students readily engage in whole-class assessment activities.
- Students can describe the status and growth of the class as a whole.
- Students seem interested in the entire class's progress.
- Students appear pleased as the whole class's performance improves.

Element 5: Using Formal Assessments of Individual Students

Formal assessments of individual students provide accurate information about their status at a particular point in time on a specific topic. To obtain such information, the teacher designs assessments based on the proficiency scale for a unit or a set of related lessons. In effect, the proficiency scale is the foundation for any and all assessments. A specific assessment might focus on all the content levels of a proficiency scale (scores 2.0, 3.0, and 4.0 content) or it might focus on only one level of a proficiency scale (such as score 2.0 content).

The various strategies that teachers might use to address this element appear in table 2.2.

Table 2.2: Using Formal Assessments of Individual Students

Strategy	Description
Common assessments designed using proficiency scales	Teachers who are responsible for the same content taught at the same level work together to design common assessments that they use to provide formative and summative feedback to students on specific topics. They then express topics as proficiency scales.
Assessments involving selected-response or short constructed-response items	The teacher creates and scores traditional assessments that employ selected-response and short constructed-response items.

Student demonstrations	The teacher asks students to generate presentations that demonstrate their understanding of a topic. Teachers typically use student demonstrations with skills, strategies, or processes.
Student interviews	The teacher holds conversations with individual students about a specific topic and then assigns each student a score that depicts his or her knowledge of the topic.
Observations of students	The teacher observes students interacting with the content and assigns a score that depicts their level of knowledge or skill regarding the specific topic observed.
Student-generated assessments	The teacher invites students to devise ways they will demonstrate competence on a particular topic at a particular level of proficiency.
Response patterns	The teacher identifies response patterns at scores 2.0, 3.0, and 4.0 as opposed to adding points to create an overall assessment score.

Source: Adapted from Marzano Resources, 2016o.

Many of the strategies in this element represent different ways to assess students. For example, common assessments are those that collaborative teams create around a specific proficiency scale (see Marzano, Heflebower, Hoegh, Warrick, & Grift, 2016). To illustrate, assume that a collaborative team of three teachers is designing a common assessment. The teachers start by creating a proficiency scale like the one in figure 2.1.

4.0	The student will be able to compare the angle sum of triangles to those of other polygons.
3.5	In addition to score 3.0 performances, the student has partial success at score 4.0 content.
3.0	The student will be able to use evidence to informally explain relationships among the angles of triangles, including the sum of interior angles and angle-angle similarity.
2.5	The student has no major errors or omissions regarding score 2.0 content, and partial success at score 3.0 content.
2.0	The student will be able to recognize and recall basic vocabulary terms such as *interior angle*, *exterior angle*, *angle sum*, *corresponding angles*, *congruent*, and *similarity*. The student will be able to recognize and recall basic facts such as the measures of the interior angles of a triangle add up to 180 degrees and when two corresponding angles of two triangles are congruent, the triangles are similar.
1.5	The student has partial success at score 2.0 content, but major errors or omissions regarding score 3.0 content.
1.0	With help, the student has partial success at score 2.0 content and score 3.0 content.
0.5	With help, the student has partial success at score 2.0 content, but not a score 3.0 content.
0.0	Even with help, the student has no success.

Source: Marzano Resources, 2016o.

Figure 2.1: Proficiency scale for common assessment.

Creating a proficiency scale is always the first order of business when designing a common assessment. As described in chapter 1, if the district has created proficiency scales for each subject area and grade level, this work is already done for collaborative teams.

The next step is to design an assessment that addresses scores 2.0, 3.0, and 4.0 content from the scale. Such an assessment appears in figure 2.2 (page 24).

The assessment in figure 2.2 includes items and tasks for score 2.0 content in section A, items and tasks for score 3.0 content in section B, and items and tasks for score 4.0 content in section C. Other assessments

Section A (Score 2.0)

1. Choose the best answer from the following options.

   When two triangles are congruent:

   a. They have the same interior and exterior sum

   b. One has an area twice as large as the other

   c. They tessellate

   d. Their corresponding sides and angles have the same length and measure

2. Fill in the blank.

   The measures of the interior angles of a triangle always add up to _____.

3. Draw lines between the corresponding angles of these triangles.

Section B (Score 3.0)

4. Determine the unknown angle measure in the following triangle. Explain how you know.

   52°

   90°

Section C (Score 4.0)

5. Use the following diagram to determine the angle sum of a convex quadrilateral. Explain your thought process.

Source: Marzano Resources, 2016o.

Figure 2.2: Assessment with three sections.

individual teachers generate might follow this same format. However, there are a variety of other forms assessments might take. For example, interviews are a type of assessment that involve teacher-led discussions during which the teacher asks questions that address level 2.0 content, level 3.0 content, and level 4.0 content. Based on students' oral responses, the teacher assigns an overall score.

Student-generated assessments are those that individual students propose and execute. This particular strategy provides maximum flexibility to students in that they can select the assessment format and form that best fit their personality and preferences.

Probably the most unusual strategy in element 5—response patterns—involves different ways of scoring assessments. To illustrate this strategy, consider figure 2.3.

Section	Item Number	Possible Points per Item	Obtained Points per Item	Section Percentage
Score 2.0	1	5	5	22/25 = 88 percent
	2	5	4	
	3	5	3	
	4	5	5	
	5	5	5	
	Total	25	22	
Score 3.0	6	10	7	15/30 = 50 percent
	7	10	4	
	8	10	4	
	Total	30	15	
Score 4.0	9	10	1	3/20 = 15 percent
	10	10	2	
	Total	20	3	

Source: Marzano Resources, 2016o.

Figure 2.3: The percentage approach to scoring assessments.

Figure 2.3 depicts an individual student's response pattern on a test that has three sections: (1) one for score 2.0 content, (2) one for score 3.0 content, and (3) one for score 4.0 content. The section for score 2.0 content contains five items that are worth five points each for a total of twenty-five points. The student obtained twenty-two of the twenty-five points for a score of 88 percent, indicating that the student knows score 2.0 content. The student acquired 50 percent of the points for score 3.0 content and only 15 percent of the points for score 4.0 content. This pattern translates into an overall score of 2.5 on the test indicating knowledge of score 2.0 content on the proficiency scale and partial knowledge of score 3.0 content.

When the strategies in this element produce the desired effects, teachers will observe the following behaviors in students.

- Students can explain what the score they received on an assessment means relative to a specific progression of knowledge.
- Students can explain what their grades mean in terms of their status in specific topics.
- Students propose ways they can demonstrate their level of proficiency on a scale.

Planning

The design question pertaining to using assessments is, How will I design and administer assessments that help students understand how their test scores and grades are related to their status on the progression of knowledge they are expected to master? The two elements that pertain to this design area provide specific guidance regarding this overall design question. Teachers can easily turn these elements into more focused planning questions.

- **Element 4:** How will I informally assess the whole class?
- **Element 5:** How will I formally assess individual students?

The teacher can address the planning question for element 4 in an opportunistic manner in that he or she might simply take advantage of situations that lend themselves to informal assessments of the whole class. For example, a teacher is conducting a lesson on level 2.0 content. She decides to employ electronic voting devices to keep track of how well students are responding to the questions. As the lesson progresses, she notices that more and more students are responding correctly to questions. She uses this information as an opportunity to celebrate the apparent growth in understanding of the class as a whole. While she could have planned for this activity, the opportunity simply presented itself, and she acted on it.

The planning question for element 5 generally requires more formal design as to the assessments teachers will administer over the course of a unit or set of related lessons. Typically, teachers like to begin a unit with a pretest that addresses scores 2.0, 3.0, and 4.0 content in the proficiency scale. They must plan for this. It is also advisable to plan for a similar post-test covering the same content but using different items and tasks. Although teachers may plan for one or more other tests to administer to students in between the pre- and post-tests, it is also advisable for the teacher to construct assessments as needed and administer them. As long as they score all assessments using the 0–4 system from the proficiency scale, teachers can compare all scores, providing a clear view of students' learning over time.

Implications for Change

The major change this design area implies is a shift from an assessment perspective to a measurement perspective. This is a veritable paradigm shift that has far-reaching implications. Currently, teachers view assessment as a series of independent activities that gather information about students' performance on a specific topic that has been the focus of instruction. Teachers score most, if not all, of these assessments using a percentage score (or some variation thereof). At some point, teachers combine all students' individual scores in some way to provide an overall score for the students on each topic. Usually, teachers use a weighted average, with scores on some tests counting more than others. They then translate the overall score to some type of overall percentage or grade.

This process tells us very little about what specific content students know and don't know. In contrast, scores teachers generate from a measurement perspective provide *explicit* knowledge about what students know and don't know. This is because a measurement approach translates scores on assessments into scores on a proficiency scale. No matter what type of assessment a teacher uses, it is always translated into the metric of a scale. For example, a teacher uses a pencil-and-paper assessment and assigns a score of 2.0 on the proficiency scale. A few days later, the teacher has a discussion with the student about score 3.0 content and concludes that the student has partial knowledge of that content. The teacher assigns a score of 2.5 on the proficiency scale based on that interaction. A week later, the teacher administers a test on the 3.0 content and concludes that the student demonstrates no major errors or omissions. Based on this assessment, the teacher assigns a score of 3.0 on the proficiency scale. This process employs a measurement perspective like that shown in figure 2.4.

Figure 2.4 indicates that assessments can take many forms, including tests, discussions, student-generated assessments, and so on. These different types of assessment might have their own specific format scores. For example, a teacher might initially score 2.0 content on a percentage basis. This percentage score is a format-specific score. Teachers can then translate format-specific scores into a score on a proficiency scale. This is the essence of the measurement process—assessments of differing formats and scoring protocols are always translated into a score on a proficiency scale. Measurements over time provide a picture of students' status at a particular time and students' growth. I believe this process allows teachers to gather more accurate, more useful information about students' status and growth than the current practice of averaging test scores.

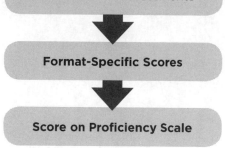

Source: *Adapted from Marzano, Norford, Finn, & Finn, in press.*

Figure 2.4: The measurement process.

CHAPTER 3

Conducting Direct Instruction Lessons

As discussed in chapter 1, the second major category in *The New Art and Science of Teaching* is *content*. This category involves strategies teachers use specifically to help students learn the information and skills that are the focus of instruction. This category includes design areas with strategies for three distinct types of lessons: (1) direct instruction, (2) practicing and deepening, and (3) knowledge application. A final design area within the content category includes those strategies applicable in all three types of lessons. Effective pedagogy is the teacher's use of the strategies within all four design areas in a coordinated fashion. In this chapter, we focus on direct instruction lessons.

In some circles, direct instruction has a tarnished reputation. It is commonly associated with didactic, lecture-oriented presentations during which students are passive consumers of information. While it is true that teachers can execute direct instruction—and all other types of instruction—in an unparticipatory manner. In fact, research continually supports the necessary role of direct instruction. Such recognition usually occurs amid loud calls for inquiry-based instruction. To illustrate, in 2011, I wrote an article in *Educational Leadership* titled "The Perils and Promises of Discovery Learning" (Marzano, 2011). There I report on a meta-analysis of 580 comparisons between discovery learning and direct instruction in which the authors (Alfieri, Broocks, Aldrich, & Tenenbaum, 2011) find that direct instruction is superior to discovery learning in most situations. As I will discuss in chapter 5, discovery learning has a place in the rotation of lesson types, but direct instruction is foundational to its success. More specifically, direct instruction is essential when teachers present new content to students.

Regarding direct instruction lessons, the desired mental states and processes in students are:

When content is new, students understand which parts are important and how the parts fit together.

The following elements are important to effective direct instruction.

Element 6: Chunking Content

When information is new to students, they best process it in small, understandable increments. This is because learners can hold only small amounts of information in their working memories (see Marzano, 1992, 2007). To illustrate, a teacher presenting students with new information about the topic of global warming might do so using a few pages from a textbook. To present the content in digestible bites—*chunks*—for students, the teacher first reads through the pages in the book, looking for natural breaks in the content. He might decide that he will have students stop after the first three paragraphs and provide time for them to reflect on the content. The next stop would be at the bottom of the page, and so on. Regardless of the form or venue, the practice is the same—the teacher halts input regarding new content at strategic points so students have time to think about what they just experienced.

The strategies within this element appear in table 3.1.

Table 3.1: Chunking Content

Strategy	Description
Using preassessment data to plan for chunks	Based on students' initial understanding of new content, the teacher presents new content in larger or smaller chunks.
Presenting content in small, sequentially related sets	The teacher chunks content into small, digestible bites for students. If presenting new declarative knowledge, the chunks comprise concepts and details that logically go together. If presenting new procedural knowledge, the chunks comprise steps in a process that go together.
Allowing for processing time between chunks	The teacher has students work together to process chunks of information.

Source: Adapted from Marzano Resources, 2016e.

Unlike strategies in most other elements, those listed for chunking are best employed sequentially. The first strategy in this element—using preassessment data to plan for chunks—deals with determining students' readiness for new content. This is important because the more students already know about content, the bigger the chunks can be; the less they know about the content, the smaller the chunks should be. A preassessment can be quite informal. For example, a preassessment about a strategy for multicolumn subtraction might simply be presenting a problem to the entire class and asking students to describe how they would approach the task. If the vast majority of students seem to understand how to approach the problem, the teacher could conclude to present the process in two sets of steps since students already seem to have a general sense of what to do. If students do not seem familiar with the process, the teacher would spend more time presenting and exemplifying individual steps. A preassessment could also be more structured and take the form of a hardcopy test that addresses the various levels of the proficiency scale.

The second strategy deals with the actual execution of the chunking process. While doing so, the teacher continually monitors the extent to which students understand the content. If the students seem confused, the teacher delves back into the content before presenting a new chunk of content.

The last strategy in table 3.1 deals with providing a structured time for students to interact about the content the teacher previously presented. This processing time is structured so that students are organized in groups and group members have specific responsibilities.

When the strategies in this element produce the desired effects, teachers will observe the following behaviors in students.

- Students actively engage in processing content between chunks.
- Students can explain why the teacher stops at specific points during a presentation of new content.
- Students appear to understand the content in each chunk.

Element 7: Processing Content

During pauses between chunks in the new content the teacher is presenting, students should be engaged in activities that help them analyze and process new information in ways that facilitate their understanding. Such processes must be well-thought-out and structured. If students simply share their thoughts about the chunk of content they just experienced, they might not interact in a way that is rigorous enough to augment their learning.

The strategies that are involved in this element appear in table 3.2.

Table 3.2: Processing Content

Strategy	Description
Perspective analysis	The teacher asks students to consider multiple perspectives on new knowledge using perspective analysis.
Thinking hats	The teacher asks students to process new information by imagining themselves wearing any one of six different-colored thinking hats representing six different types of perspectives: white hat (neutral and objective perspectives), red hat (emotional perspectives), black hat (cautious or careful perspectives), yellow hat (optimistic perspectives), green hat (creative perspectives), and blue hat (organizational perspectives) (de Bono, 1999).
Collaborative processing	The teacher asks students to meet in small groups to summarize the information he or she just presented, ask clarifying questions about the information, and make predictions about upcoming information.
Jigsaw cooperative learning	The teacher organizes students in teams of equal size (for example, four members) and the content into as many categories as there are team members (for example, four categories). The teacher assigns individual team members to each content chunk to become experts. They then return to their teams to present their content.
Reciprocal teaching	After the teacher presents the chunk of content, the discussion leader in a group asks questions about the information presented, and the group members discuss each question. Someone from the group summarizes the content presented so far, and the group members make predictions about the upcoming chunk of content, beginning the cycle again.
Concept attainment	The teacher asks students to identify, compare, and contrast examples and nonexamples of a concept.
Think-pair-share	The teacher asks students to think critically about a question, pair up with another classmate to come to a consensus on their answer to the question, and then share their response with other groups or the whole class.
Scripted cooperative dyads	Students take notes about the main idea and key details of new content. The teacher breaks students into groups of two and assigns each student to act either as the recaller or the listener. The recaller summarizes the content without looking at his or her notes, while the listener adds missing information and corrects any errors in the recaller's summary. Students switch roles during the next chunk.

Source: Adapted from Marzano Resources, 2016bb.

All the strategies in table 3.2 focus on helping students process the content in such a way as to increase their comprehension and retention. However, they do so in different ways. Two of the strategies—perspective analysis and thinking hats—require students to think about the content in unusual ways. For example, perspective analysis requires students to identify their own position on a topic and the reasoning supporting it. Students next consider a different position on the topic and the reasoning behind it.

A few strategies provide very specific procedures for how students are to process the content. For example, the jigsaw strategy requires students to meet in groups to become local experts on specific aspects of the new content being presented. Local experts then report back to their original groups, sharing what they have learned.

Some of the strategies focus more on the collaboration process. For example, the strategy of scripted cooperative dyads requires students to interact from the perspective of one of two roles: (1) recaller and (2) listener. Students continually shift roles, providing for a systematic dialogue about the new content.

When the strategies in this element produce the desired effects, teachers will observe the following behaviors in students.

- Students appear to be actively interacting with the content.
- Students volunteer predictions.
- Students can explain what they have just learned.
- Students voluntarily ask clarification questions.

Element 8: Recording and Representing Content

The final element important to direct instruction lessons involves providing students with opportunities to record and represent the content that has been the focus of the lesson. The end goal of such activities is that students create an internal representation of the content. In technical terms, students *encode* the content in ways that are personally meaningful. There are two basic ways to encode information: linguistically and nonlinguistically (Marzano, 1992, 2007). *Linguistic* representation involves using language to encode new content. For example, students are representing content linguistically when they write a summary about what they have just learned or when they create a word web that includes the key parts of the content. They are representing content *nonlinguistically* when they create graphic organizers and make pictorial models. Strategies within this element appear in table 3.3.

Table 3.3: Recording and Representing Content

Strategy	Description
Informal outlines	The teacher has students use indentation to indicate the relative importance of ideas. They write big ideas at the left side of the paper, and indent and list details under the big idea to which they pertain.
Summaries	The teacher asks students to summarize content briefly and quickly. Summaries focus on identifying the critical content and describing how the pieces fit together.
Pictorial notes and pictographs	The teacher asks students to use pictorial notes and pictographs to illustrate new content. Pictorial notes may serve as an accompaniment to written notes or, in some cases, as the primary note-taking form.
Combination notes, pictures, and summaries	The teacher has students record notes about the content in a chart's left column, draw pictographs or pictorial representations of the content in the right column, and write a brief summary of the content in the lower section of the chart.

Strategy	Description
Graphic organizers	The teacher has students record their knowledge using graphic organizers that correspond to specific patterns commonly found in information. Common text structures include sequence, description, comparison, causation, and problem and solution.
Free-flowing webs	The teacher has students place big ideas in central circles and then use lines to connect big ideas to smaller circles with important details about each big idea. Unlike a simple description graphic organizer, a free-flowing web connects multiple subtopics by showing how they relate to a central topic.
Academic notebooks	The teacher has students record their notes in a permanent record to which they add new notes and make corrections to their thinking as they review previous entries.
Dramatic enactments	The teacher has students role-play characters or act out scenes, processes, or events. They can also use their bodies to create symbols for concepts such as radius, diameter, and circumference.
Mnemonic devices	A teacher uses mnemonic devices to help students remember, record, and represent critical content. Mnemonic devices often link content to symbols, imagery, and patterns of sound to strengthen the user's memory.
Rhyming pegwords	The teacher has students use a set of concrete images that rhyme with the numbers one through ten, such as one is a bun, two is a shoe, and so on. Students then form mental pictures of content they wish to recall with the concrete images. The strategy allows students to memorize content presented as lists.
Link strategies	The teacher has students create symbols or substitutes for important ideas and then link together those symbols or substitutes in a narrative. A symbol is an image that reminds one of important information, like a rainbow to represent the concept of an arc. A substitute is a word that is easy to picture and sounds like the information one is trying to remember, like the word ark (a big boat) to remember the concept of the arc of a circle.

Source: Adapted from Marzano Resources, 2016gg.

Some of the strategies in table 3.3 focus on encoding content linguistically. For example, an informal outline uses indentations to signify the importance of summary statements about content. Some strategies focus on encoding content nonlinguistically. For example, pictorial notes and pictographs employ symbols and sketches to represent content. Some strategies like combination notes, pictures, and summaries employ linguistic and nonlinguistic representations simultaneously. Some strategies involve techniques that enhance students' abilities to recall the content. For example, students can use mnemonic devices, rhyming pegwords, and link strategies as memory aids. Academic notebooks is an overarching strategy in that they can house almost any type of linguistic or nonlinguistic representation.

When the strategies in this element produce the desired effects, teachers will observe the following behaviors in students.

- Students produce summaries that include critical information.
- Students produce nonlinguistic representations that include critical information.
- Students can explain their linguistic and nonlinguistic representations.
- Students remember the critical content from previous lessons.

Planning

The design question pertaining to conducting direct instruction lessons is, When content is new, how will I design and deliver direct instruction lessons that help students understand which parts are important and how the parts fit together? The three elements that pertain to this design area provide specific guidance regarding this overall design question. Teachers can easily turn these elements into more focused planning questions.

- **Element 6:** How will I chunk the new content into short, digestible bites?
- **Element 7:** How will I help students process the individual chunks and the content as a whole?
- **Element 8:** How will I help students record and represent their knowledge?

The planning issue teachers must address first is the content to focus on during direct instruction. This is an important consideration because not all content is important enough to warrant the time necessary for a direct instruction lesson. As discussed in chapters 1 and 2, a proficiency scale is a powerful tool to this end. By definition, the content a proficiency scale articulates represents that which is important enough to warrant direct instruction. To illustrate, consider the proficiency scale in figure 3.1.

4.0	The student will engage in a projective investigation task where he or she projects and defends what might have happened if the women's suffrage movement had failed.
3.5	In addition to score 3.0 performance, the student has partial success at score 4.0 content.
3.0	The students will understand implications of women's suffrage in the United States (early 20th century) and implications of the African-American civil rights movement (1955–1968).
2.5	There are no major errors or omissions regarding score 2.0 content, and the student has partial success at score 3.0 content.
2.0	The student will be able to recognize and recall basic vocabulary terms such as *economic imperialism*, *nationalism*, and *militarism*. The student will be able to recognize and recall basic facts such as: • The Nineteenth Amendment was proposed on June 4, 1919 and ratified on August 18, 1920. • Martin Luther King Jr., delivered his "I Have a Dream" speech on August 28, 1963 from the steps of the Lincoln Memorial.
1.5	The student has partial success at score 2.0 content, but major errors or omissions regarding score 3.0 content.
1.0	With help, the student has partial success at score 2.0 content and score 3.0 content.
0.5	With help, the student has partial success at score 2.0 content, but not at score 3.0 content.
0.0	Even with help, the student has no success.

Figure 3.1: Social studies proficiency scale.

Levels 2.0, 3.0, and 4.0 content all have components that deserve direct instruction. At the 2.0 level, the teacher would use direct instruction strategies to introduce students to vocabulary, such as *economic imperialism*, *nationalism*, and *militarism*. He or she would also use direct instruction to introduce details like the Nineteenth Amendment was proposed on June 4, 1919, and ratified on August 18, 1920, and Martin Luther King Jr. delivered his "I Have a Dream" speech on August 28, 1963, from the steps of the Lincoln Memorial. At the 3.0 level, the teacher would use direct instruction to exemplify the relationship between woman suffrage and the civil rights movement. Even the 4.0 level could benefit from direct instruction. For example, direct instruction might be required to teach students the process of projective investigation.

Implications for Change

The major implication for change regarding this design area is that direct instruction lessons should be well-crafted and polished creations. As we have seen, direct instruction lessons can apply to all three levels of explicit content in a proficiency scale. Such lessons are not easy to create. In fact, a well-designed direct instruction lesson typically goes through a series of revisions before it produces optimal results. This makes direct instruction lessons perfect candidates for lesson study.

Lesson study is best executed in the context of collaborative teams as part of the PLC process (DuFour, DuFour, Eaker, Many, & Mattos, 2016; see also Marzano et al., 2016). Specifically, a collaborative team working within the context of a PLC selects a unit of instruction and creates a common proficiency scale articulating scores 2.0, 3.0, and 4.0 content on the scale. As is traditional practice, collaborative team members create a common pretest and post-test using the scale. Additionally, collaborative team members identify content at scores 2.0, 3.0, and 4.0 that will require direct instruction lessons.

Some of these lessons might be relatively detailed as is the case when score 2.0 content involves many vocabulary terms and details. In other situations, the direct instruction lesson might be quite short, as is the case when score 4.0 content requires the introduction of a few details or additions to previously presented concepts so that students might engage in a knowledge application task.

After identifying content that requires direct instruction lessons, the team would perhaps rely on more experienced teachers to take the lead in lesson design. Team members then try out these lessons and seek input from the team, ideally through direct observation or video recordings. Team members then revise and retry lessons until they consistently produce desired results in students.

Over time, a school or district develops an archived set of direct instruction lessons for the various content levels of its proficiency scales. The school or district can continually update and augment the lessons by adding new activities and resources teachers might use when they deliver these well-vetted lessons. Lesson study, when conducted in this fashion, creates a growing set of resources that helps teachers in arguably the most labor-intensive type of lesson: direct instruction.

CHAPTER 4

Conducting Practicing and Deepening Lessons

Once content is introduced through direct instruction, teachers must further develop student knowledge.

> The desired mental states and processes for students
> for lessons designed to develop knowledge are:
>
> After teachers present new content, students deepen their
> understanding and develop fluency with skills and processes.

When conducting practicing and deepening lessons, it is important to keep in mind the difference between procedural and declarative knowledge. *Procedural knowledge* includes skills, strategies, and processes. For example, converting fractions to decimals is a skill because it requires a set of steps usually performed in a specific order. Decoding is a strategy because it involves specific actions although they are not necessarily performed in the same order each time. Writing an expository essay is a process because it involves executing multiple strategies that have different outcomes but must work together in a unified manner.

Declarative knowledge involves information. It too comes in a variety of forms. At the lowest level, it involves knowledge of terminology. For example, *interior angle*, *similarity*, *congruence*, and *angle measure* might be recognizable as terms. The next level includes facts. Facts might include specific characteristics of congruence and similarity. Both terminology and facts are relatively specific and together are referred to as *details*. At a much broader level are generalizations and principles. They organize terms and facts into related sets of information. Generalizations describe the angles of a triangle including the sum of interior angles and angle-angle similarity and congruence. Principles describe the relationship between variables; for example, as one variable increases, the other decreases. At the highest level of organization are concepts. They organize generalizations and principles into bigger systems of information. For example, the concept of *polygon* can organize generalizations, principles, and details about triangles, rectangles, trapezoids, and the like.

The following elements are important to effective practicing and deepening lessons.

Element 9: Using Structured Practice Sessions

Practice is a staple of effective teaching, but it is commonly misunderstood. One obvious consideration is that practice applies to procedural knowledge, not declarative knowledge. That is, students need to practice skills, strategies, and processes. They do not need to practice details, generalizations, principles, and concepts. Rather, students deepen such declarative knowledge through other types of activities addressed in this chapter like examining similarities and differences.

Another consideration is that all procedural knowledge progresses through three stages: (1) cognitive, (2) associative, and (3) autonomous (see Anderson, 1983; Fitts & Posner, 1967). At the *cognitive stage*, students are simply learning about the skill, strategy, or process. At this point, they are learning declarative knowledge. For example, when a teacher is first explaining and demonstrating a strategy for reading a bar graph, it is simply information to students. Students aren't executing anything at this stage. Rather, they are trying to understand what you do first, what you do next, and so on.

At the *associative stage*, students are trying out the strategy and determining which parts they have to alter or augment to make the strategy efficient and effective for them personally. This is the phase that requires the most analysis by students since they have to determine which parts of the procedure they might change. Finally, at the *autonomous phase*, students are fine tuning their ability to execute the procedure and developing fluency in its use.

The specific strategies that relate to this element appear in table 4.1.

Table 4.1: Using Structured Practice Sessions

Strategy	Description
Modeling	When presenting any skill, strategy, or process to students, the teacher first models it for them. This involves the teacher walking through the steps involved in the skill, strategy, or process and thinking aloud as he or she does so.
Guided practice	The teacher provides well-structured opportunities for students to practice new skills, strategies, or processes. During these opportunities, activities move from very simple to more complex versions of the skill, strategy, or process.
Close monitoring	The teacher provides a highly structured practice environment and monitors students' actions very closely to correct early errors or misunderstandings.
Frequent structured practice	The teacher first provides a clear demonstration of the skill or process. After this demonstration, the teacher provides frequent opportunities to practice discrete elements of the skill or process and the skill or process as a whole in situations where students have a high probability of success.
Varied practice	The teacher provides opportunities to practice a skill or process in more challenging situations. Students still experience success, but they might be required to work a bit harder than was necessary during frequent structured practice.
Fluency practice	The teacher engages students in independent practice in which they focus on performing the skill or process skillfully, accurately, quickly, and automatically.
Worked examples	While students are practicing skills or processes, the teacher provides them with problems or examples that have already been worked out so they receive a clear image of the correct procedure.
Practice sessions prior to testing	The teacher sets up a practice schedule to ensure that students have a chance to review and practice skills or processes before they are tested or retested on them.

Source: Adapted from Marzano Resources, 2016kk.

The strategies in table 4.1 cover the spectrum of procedural knowledge development. Teachers commonly use modeling when introducing a new skill, strategy, or process. During modeling, the teacher describes the procedure and walks through the steps so students can observe them as they are executed. As discussed earlier, students will be at the cognitive stage of procedural development when teachers present a new procedure; students are trying to understand what the procedure is intended to accomplish and how it's done.

Students use many strategies in table 4.1 as they advance through the associative phase by practicing the various parts and making alterations. One of the most powerful strategies to employ during the associative phase of learning is worked examples. As the name implies, this strategy involves showing students concrete examples of what it looks like when a skill is executed well. To illustrate, consider the skill of translating fractions into decimals. While designing a practice activity for students, the teacher includes some step-by-step examples of how to turn fractions into decimals with comments to ensure that students understand each step. Some of the strategies are best during the autonomous phase. Fluency practice is clearly one of these. At this stage, practice focuses on speed and accuracy with the procedure.

One strategy within this element that often elicits questions from teachers is practice sessions prior to testing. There is a common misconception that once a student has reached a level of fluency with a skill, strategy, or process, he or she can maintain that level of proficiency without any further effort. In fact, if a student has not used a skill, strategy, or process in a while, the student should have the opportunity to practice it before being tested on its use.

When the strategies in this element produce the desired effects, teachers will observe the following behaviors in students.

- Students actively engage in practice activities.
- Students ask questions about the procedure.
- Students increase their competence with the procedure.
- Students increase their confidence in their ability to execute the procedure.
- Students increase their fluency in executing the procedure.

Element 10: Examining Similarities and Differences

This element helps students deepen their understanding of declarative knowledge by examining how things are alike and not alike. Strategies within this element apply to both declarative and procedural knowledge. Consider the concepts of supply and demand, which are clearly declarative in nature. Students might be asked to identify and articulate characteristics that are common to both concepts and unique to each concept. This would most likely deepen their understanding of both. The same holds true for procedural knowledge when students are first learning it. Recall that when students are in the cognitive stage they are learning the procedure as information. When this is the case, it is useful to have students examine the similarities and differences between the procedure they are learning newly and a procedure they have already learned. For example, if a teacher is introducing students to the procedure for multicolumn subtraction, it would be useful to have them examine its similarities and differences with the procedure of multicolumn addition, which they learned previously.

A wide variety of strategies foster students deepening their knowledge by examining similarities and differences. These strategies appear in table 4.2 (page 40).

Table 4.2: Examining Similarities and Differences

Strategy	Description
Sentence-stem comparisons	The teacher has students complete sentence stems that ask them to compare and contrast various people, places, events, concepts, or processes: House cats are similar to lions because _____. House cats are different than lions because _____.
Summaries	The teacher has students summarize similarities and differences using three columns: (1) the left column lists features that are only found in the first item, (2) the far right column lists features that are only found in the second item, and (3) the middle column lists features that are similar between the two items and includes a sentence that summarizes the items' similarities.
Constructed-response comparisons	The teacher has students describe, in a short paragraph, how items are similar or different. This strategy begins with a simple teacher request: "How is _____ similar to and different from _____?" Students must decide which similarities and differences to include in their responses and how to best frame their analyses.
Venn diagrams	The teacher asks students to compare and contrast elements using overlapping circles. Students write similarities where circles intersect, and they write characteristics unique to the comparison items where the circles do not intersect.
T-charts	The teacher has students use T-charts to compare two objects, ideas, events, or people. Students fill in a T-shaped graphic organizer by writing two topics across the top and details that describe each on either side of a dividing line. Once students have gathered several characteristics for each item, they look for similarities and differences between the two items.
Double-bubble diagrams	The teacher has students write two items to compare in large circles on the left and right sides of a page. They list common attributes in smaller circles in the center of the page that connect to both large circles. They write unique attributes in smaller circles at the edges of the page that connect only to the larger circle to which they apply.
Comparison matrices	The teacher has students write elements they wish to compare at the top of each column in a matrix. In the rows, students write the characteristics on which they will compare the elements. Then, in each cell, students record information related to each attribute for each element. Finally, students summarize what they have learned by comparing the elements.
Classification charts	The teacher creates a chart with several categories listed across the top and asks students to fill in examples that fit in each category.
Dichotomous keys	The teacher has students focus on differences between elements by using dichotomous keys. A dichotomous key is a graphic organizer that refines students' understanding of two or more items by delineating different characteristics of each. Thus, the items should have relatively obvious similarities. The strategy is useful for distinguishing between similar organisms in science, but the teachers can adapt it for any subject that requires students to distinguish among items in the same category.
Sorting, matching, and categorizing	The teacher asks students to sort, match, and categorize content. When sorting, students place items into specific, predetermined categories. When matching, students match two things that are equivalent to one another. When categorizing, students group elements into two or more categories and explain the reasoning behind their categorization.
Similes	The teacher asks students to state comparisons using *like* or *as*: Adding fractions with different denominators is like trying to add apples and oranges.
Metaphors	The teacher asks students to state comparisons as direct relationships—where one thing is another: Life is a journey.
Sentence-stem analogies	The teacher has students use sentence stems to create comparisons that describe specific relationships between two items or concepts. Analogies take the following form: "Item one is to item two as item three is to item four." Quarterback is to _____ as pitcher is to _____.
Visual analogies	The teacher asks students to use visual organizers to help them make analogies. The organizer has two parallel lines, one above the other, each with a bisecting line in the middle. The student writes the first pair of elements in the analogy on the top line and the second pair on the bottom line. In between the lines, students describe the relationship connecting the two pairs of elements.

Source: Adapted from Marzano Resources, 2016n.

The strategies in table 4.2 represent different ways to have students examine similarities and differences between elements. There are fourteen strategies within this element; therefore, a teacher could engage students in a great deal of knowledge-deepening activities involving similarities and differences without repeating any given strategy. Some of the strategies involve the use of specific graphic organizers like Venn diagrams, T-charts, double-bubble diagrams, and comparison matrices. Some involve the identification of abstract characteristics like similes, metaphors, and analogies. Some strategies, like classification charts, sorting, matching, categorizing, and student-generated classification patterns involve variations on how one might define similarities and differences.

When the strategies in this element produce the desired effects, teachers will observe the following behaviors in students.

- Students understand the similarities and differences between the elements being compared.
- Students ask questions about the similarities and differences between the elements being compared.
- Students can explain how the activities deepened their knowledge.

Element 11: Examining Errors in Reasoning

This element helps deepen students' understanding of content by having them examine their own reasoning or the overall logic of information presented to them. Such activities are at the core of what is referred to as *college and career readiness* (Conley, 2014). This makes intuitive sense in that students who are ready for college and careers have the ability to analyze their own or others' thinking.

Specific strategies within this element appear in table 4.3.

Table 4.3: Examining Errors in Reasoning

Strategy	Description
Identifying errors of faulty logic	The teacher asks students to find and analyze errors of faulty logic. Errors of faulty logic refer to situations in which sound reasons do not support a conclusion. Specific types of errors in this category include contradiction, accident, false cause, composition, division, begging the question, evading the issue, and arguing from ignorance.
Identifying errors of attack	The teacher asks students to find and analyze errors of attack. Errors of attack happen when a person focuses on the context of an argument, rather than the argument itself, in trying to refute the other side.
Identifying errors of weak reference	The teacher asks students to find and analyze errors of weak reference. Specific types of these errors include using sources that reflect biases, using sources that lack credibility, appealing to authority, appealing to the people, and appealing to emotion.
Identifying errors of misinformation	The teacher asks students to find and analyze errors of misinformation. Two types of misinformation errors are confusing the facts and misapplying a concept or generalization.
Practicing identifying errors in logic	The teacher uses practice exercises to help students identify errors in logic. Typically, these exercises will describe a scenario in a few sentences and ask students to identify the reasoning error present in the scenario. Students might select the answer in a multiple choice or matching format or be asked to recall the answer from memory.
Finding errors in the media	The teacher provides students with footage of political debates, televised interviews, commercials, advertisements, newspaper articles, blogs, and other sources and asks them to find and analyze errors in reasoning that underlie the messages therein.
Examining support for claims	The teacher asks students to examine the support provided for a claim by analyzing the grounds, backing, and qualifiers that support it. Grounds are the reasons given to support a claim and backing is the evidence, facts, or data that support the grounds, while qualifiers address exceptions or objections to the claim.

continued →

Strategy	Description
Judging reasoning and evidence in an author's work	The teacher asks students to apply their knowledge of reasoning and argumentation to delineate and evaluate the arguments present in a text. Students read a text and identify the claim, grounds, backing, and qualifiers. Students must decide whether the reasoning is valid or logical (containing no errors) and whether the supporting evidence is sufficient and relevant.
Identifying statistical limitations	The teacher asks students to find and analyze errors that commonly occur when using statistical data to support a claim. The five major types of statistical limitations for students to be aware of are: (1) regression toward the mean, (2) conjunction, (3) base rates, (4) the limits of extrapolation, and (5) the cumulative nature of probabilistic events.
Using student-friendly prompts	The teacher phrases prompts and questions in nontechnical language to trigger students to look for certain types of errors; for example, asking students to look for "getting off topic" rather than "evading the issue."
Anticipating student errors	The teacher identifies errors that students are likely to make during a lesson. When presenting content, the teacher alerts students to the potential problems. For example, when a teacher introduces the process for finding the area of a right triangle, he or she reminds students it is sometimes difficult to identify the base and height if the triangle has been rotated.
Avoiding unproductive habits of mind	Unproductive habits of mind are those that hinder us from completing complex tasks. To counteract unproductive habits, the teacher reinforces the following productive habits of mind: staying focused when answers and solutions are not immediately apparent, pushing the limits of your knowledge and skills, generating and pursuing your own standards of excellence, seeking incremental steps, accuracy, and clarity, resisting impulsivity, and seeking cohesion and coherence.

Source: Adapted from Marzano Resources, 2016m.

The strategies in table 4.3 address a wide variety of ways teachers can aid students in examining their reasoning or that of others. Some of the strategies involve recognizing and rectifying specific types of errors: identifying faulty logic, errors of attack, errors of weak reference, errors of misinformation, and errors in logic. Teachers have used these strategies since the 1950s (Toulmin, 1958). Other strategies involve relatively new reasoning skills that have become salient in the literature since the mid-1990s (see Marzano, 1992). To illustrate, consider habits of mind. A *habit of mind* (also known as a *mental disposition*) is a habitual way we have of thinking in complex situations. Some habits of mind render our thinking ineffective. For example, an unproductive habit is to give up as soon as you realize you don't have an obvious or immediate solution to a problem or an answer to a question. Each unproductive habit of mind has a related productive habit of mind that renders our thinking highly efficient and effective. In this case, the productive habit of mind would be staying focused when answers and solutions are not immediately apparent. Some of the strategies for this element focus students' attention on the errors that might be found in specific situations, such as finding errors in the media or in an author's work.

When the strategies in this element produce the desired effects, teachers will observe the following behaviors in students.

- Students actively identify and analyze their own errors.
- Students actively identify and analyze others' errors.
- Students can describe and exemplify the different types of errors one might make.
- Students can explain how the activities have increased their understanding of the content.

Planning

The design question pertaining to practicing and deepening lessons is: After presenting new content, how will I design and deliver lessons that help students deepen their understanding and develop fluency in skills and processes? The three elements that pertain to this design area provide specific guidance regarding this overall design question. Teachers can easily turn these elements into more focused planning questions.

- **Element 9:** How will I help students engage in structured practice?
- **Element 10:** How will I help students examine similarities and differences?
- **Element 11:** How will I help students examine errors in reasoning?

These three specific planning questions represent distinct types of activities. They imply no specific sequence. To plan, a teacher must consider the specific types of content that are the focus of instruction. If content is procedural, then structured practice is a necessity. For example, if a unit or set of lessons focuses on the process of translating primary data into a specific type of graph, the teacher plans strategies that ensure students move through all three stages of development for procedural knowledge: (1) the cognitive stage, (2) the associative stage, and (3) the autonomous stage.

If the focus of the unit or set of lessons is more declarative in nature, examining similarities and differences is the lead strategy from which to plan. For example, if the focus of the unit deals with the generalization that the tilt and revolution of the Earth around the sun affects the seasons, the teacher might plan for a few activities like having students create a double-bubble diagram depicting the predicted similarities and differences in weather at a specific location on Earth when the tilt is at two diametrically opposed angles.

Finally, the teacher might plan for one or more activities that involve analyzing errors. For procedural content, the errors might simply focus on mistakes that are common when translating primary data into a specific type of graph. On the declarative side, the errors might focus on the habit of mind of seeking accuracy.

Implications for Change

The major implication for change regarding practicing and deepening lessons is that teachers must directly teach new sets of skills—other than academic content—directly to students. These include errors of attack, faulty logic, weak reference, misinformation, statistical limitations, and unproductive habits of mind. Each of these involves complex content that requires instruction in its own right. To illustrate, consider the error of faulty logic. Some specific types of faulty logic errors are defined in figure 4.1.

Contradiction: Presenting conflicting information; for example, saying that downloading music illegally should be punished more harshly while also arguing that Internet providers and the government shouldn't be allowed to collect information about Internet users

Accident: Failing to recognize that an argument is based on an exception to a rule; for example, if a person argues that Scotland has a warm and sunny climate based on the weather during her one-week vacation there

False cause: Confusing a temporal (time) order of events with causality or oversimplifying the reasons behind some event or occurrence; for example, superstitious beliefs such as wearing a certain shirt so that your favorite team will win

Begging the question: Making a claim and then arguing for the claim by using statements that are simply the equivalent of the original claim; for example, saying that Namibia is the most beautiful country because it has the prettiest landscape

Evading the issue: Changing the topic to avoid addressing the issue; for example, if a student defends himself against accusations of cheating on a test by saying that he always does his homework and never breaks curfew

Arguing from ignorance: Arguing that a claim is justified simply because its opposite has not been proven true; for example, claiming that a certain subatomic particle must not exist because we haven't discovered it yet

Composition: Asserting something about a whole that is true of only its parts; for example, creating a stereotype about a whole group of people based on the actions or traits of a few people from that group

Division: Making a claim about individual parts based on the fact that it is generally true of the whole; for example, saying that because you dislike sandwiches, you must dislike tomatoes

---

Source: Marzano Resources, 2016m.

Figure 4.1: Errors of faulty logic.

Figure 4.1 lists common errors that occur in a wide variety of situations, both formal and informal. Before students can recognize these errors, they must understand them. This implies that the teacher has to explain the errors and provide students with practice identifying them. Specifically, the teacher spends an adequate amount of time providing the class with examples of these types of fallacies and eliciting examples from students. Next, the teacher presents students with exercises like the one in figure 4.2.

1. Connor's family has a dog that is almost twenty years old. When his friend's dog dies, Connor asks his mom how it could have happened. "His dog was only twelve," Connor says. "He should have lived a lot longer."

2. Jamie and Lewis are discussing the AIDS epidemic. "Maybe someday they'll find a cure," Jamie says. "There is no cure for AIDS," Lewis says. "They haven't found one yet, have they? And they've tried for a long time. That means there is no cure."

3. James is working on an essay for class, and Jamal asks him why he is writing it out by hand instead of using the computer. James says that the last time he used the computer he got a bad grade, so now he writes everything by hand first and types it on the computer later.

4. Annabelle and Zelda are assigned to debate whether or not Woodrow Wilson was a good U.S. president. Zelda goes first and presents her argument for why Wilson was a good president. When it is Annabelle's turn to speak, she begins by saying, "Since you all know Zelda, you'll understand that she is wrong, because she is always so rude."

5. Taylor asks Gale why she is wearing a jacket with a hole in the elbow. Gale tells him it is the new style. "Look around," she says. "Everyone is doing it."

6. Sasha has written a paper about the presidency of Ronald Reagan. Her teacher notices that most of the people Sasha quotes in the paper said that he was an excellent president. Almost all of them are from people who worked very closely with him, and the quotes were recorded when they were still working for him.

7. Lawrence says he wants to get a master's degree in business administration after going to college, and Charlotte says she thinks that's great. "What kind of business do you want to go into?" she asks. Lawrence replies, "I don't want to go into business, I just want to make more money. People with MBAs make more money."

Answers: 1—Accident; 2—Arguing from ignorance; 3—False cause; 4—Arguing against the person; 5—Appealing to the people; 6—Using sources that reflect bias; 7—Misapplying a concept or generalization

Source: Marzano Resources, 2016m.

Figure 4.2: Exercise for errors in reasoning.

The various productive habits of mind also require instruction and practice. Again, the teacher must provide examples and elicit examples from students. Additionally, the teacher would have to provide guidance as to the type of situation in which specific habits of mind apply. This is summarized in table 4.4.

Table 4.4: Situations in Which Habits of Mind Apply

Habit of Mind	Situation	Self-Analysis Question
Staying focused when answers and solutions are not immediately apparent	You are trying to solve a problem that is very difficult.	Am I giving up because I can't find the answer right away?
Pushing the limits of your knowledge and skills	You are working on a complex project or goal that takes a long time.	Am I stopping because I have to acquire new knowledge or skills to accomplish this?
Generating and pursuing your own standards of excellence	You are working on a complex project or goal that takes a long time.	Have I identified what the final product should look like in order for me to feel that I have done my best?

Seeking incremental steps	You are working on a complex project or goal that takes a long time.	Am I breaking the big project into small pieces that I can more easily accomplish?
Seeking accuracy	You are seeing, hearing, or learning something new.	Am I doing something or asking questions to determine if the new information is accurate?
Seeking clarity	You are seeing, hearing, or learning something new.	Am I aware of when I'm getting confused and stopping to ask questions or do something to clarify things?
Resisting impulsivity	You have to make a decision or react to something.	Am I aware that I'm acting without thinking about my actions and then stopping for a moment to examine my conclusions?
Seeking cohesion and coherence	You are creating something that has a lot of related parts.	Am I making sure that all the pieces fit together and work toward a common goal?

Source: Marzano Resources, 2016m.

As table 4.4 illustrates, productive habits of mind cut across a wide range of activities. To provide practice in these habits of mind, teachers have to make these activities available to students. For example, consider the productive habit of staying focused when answers and solutions are not immediately apparent. To provide students with practice, teachers design opportunities for students to solve very difficult problems with the expressed purpose of practicing this disposition.

I believe that the college- and career-readiness skills embedded in this design area represent a new curriculum that teachers must cover in concert with academic content. Chapter 11 (page 103) discusses this change in depth.

CHAPTER 5

Conducting Knowledge Application Lessons

A third type of content lesson a teacher might employ involves knowledge application.

> The desired mental states and processes for students are:
>
> After the presentation of new content, students generate and defend claims through knowledge application tasks.

Knowledge application lessons engage students in activities that require them to apply what they have learned in unique situations. As discussed in chapter 3, knowledge application lessons are where discovery learning activities make the most sense. However, the discovery learning teachers execute during knowledge application lessons is not pure discovery, where students are pretty much left to their own devices in their exploration of specific declarative or procedural knowledge. Such *unassisted discovery* is highly ineffective (see Alfieri et al., 2011). In contrast, *enhanced discovery* is a very powerful instructional tool. *Enhanced discovery* involves the scaffolding of content from the direct instruction lessons and the practicing and deepening lessons in chapters 3 and 4 respectively. First, students learn the content as a result of well-planned direct instruction lessons and practicing and deepening lessons. Then, they engage in discovery processes.

The following elements are important to effective knowledge application lessons.

Element 12: Engaging Students in Cognitively Complex Tasks

By definition, cognitively complex tasks require a number of mental steps for students. They also require using content in new ways. The specific strategies that relate to this element appear in table 5.1 (page 48).

Table 5.1: Engaging Students in Cognitively Complex Tasks

Strategy	Description
Experimental-inquiry tasks	The teacher has students use experimental-inquiry tasks to make predictions, test them, examine the results, evaluate the results, and reflect on the process to come to a defensible conclusion. Observations, experiments, surveys, and interviews are all appropriate data-collection techniques for this type of task.
Problem-solving tasks	The teacher has students use problem-solving tasks to set a goal, identify obstacles or constraints to reaching that goal, find solutions, predict which solution is most likely to work, test their prediction, examine the results, evaluate the results, and reflect on the process.
Tasks to examine the efficiencies of multiple methods of problem solving	The teacher has students use logic to evaluate multiple methods of problem solving. Students determine which method is most effective or efficient by comparing aspects of each.
Decision-making tasks	The teacher has students use decision-making tasks to identify possible alternatives, outline the criteria for which each alternative will be judged, apply the criteria to each alternative, and select the most appropriate alternative.
Investigation tasks	The teacher has students use investigation tasks to identify a concept, past event, or future hypothetical event to be investigated; identify what is already known about the subject of investigation; identify confusions or contradictions; and develop a plausible resolution to the confusions or contradictions.
Invention tasks	The teacher has students design a product that achieves a specific goal, solves a problem, or makes a task easier. Students consider what design will best suit the purposes and requirements of the task and then develop a prototype. Students then test the prototype in order to determine how effectively it meets their expectations and if it can be improved.
Student-designed tasks	The teacher asks students to design a task that deepens their understanding of a topic that interests them and relates to the class's learning target or unit. This is done when students are comfortable performing the various types of cognitively complex tasks.

Source: Adapted from Marzano Resources, 2016k.

The strategies in table 5.1 involve steps that require students to think deeply about content. To illustrate, consider the cognitively complex task of experimental inquiry. It addresses the following questions.

- What is my prediction?
- How will I test my prediction?
- What do I expect to see if my prediction is correct?
- What actually happened?
- Did my prediction come true?
- How has my thinking changed?
- What conclusions can I defend?

Cognitively complex tasks also require students to apply what they have learned in novel situations—hence the term *knowledge application lessons*. For example, assume that students in an art class were exposed to certain design principles during one or more direct instruction lessons and knowledge-deepening lessons. At the knowledge application level, the teacher might assign the following experimental inquiry task:

> Select three different visual structures that, according to the design principles we've been studying, can have different effects on the viewer, such as a sense of balance, anxiety, or rhythm. Create simple drawings that you believe exemplify each structure and find out if you are successful in communicating what you intend. For example, survey your classmates to tell you which drawing represents which effect. Decide if, based on the results, you can change the design to improve your results. (Marzano & Kendall, 2008, p. 106)

This task requires students to create an original composition, survey viewers' reactions, analyze the data, and draw conclusions.

When the strategies in this element produce the desired effects, teachers will observe the following behaviors in students.

- Students are clearly engaged in their cognitively complex task.
- Students can explain the conclusions they have generated.
- Students can defend their conclusions.
- Students have produced artifacts from their cognitively complex task.

Element 13: Providing Resources and Guidance

This category of strategies involves actions teachers take to help students as they engage in their cognitively complex tasks. During such tasks, the teacher's role shifts from providing new content (which is his or her role during direct instruction) or orchestrating the ways students are analyzing content (which is his or her role during practicing and deepening lessons) to providing support as students work with some relative independence on knowledge application tasks. The strategies associated with this element appear in table 5.2.

Table 5.2: Providing Resources and Guidance

Strategy	Description
Using proficiency or scoring scales	The teacher asks students to use a proficiency or scoring scale to monitor their progress toward a learning goal over the course of a cognitively complex task. These scales relate to student progress on complex tasks as opposed to academic content.
Providing resources	When asking students to complete a cognitively complex task, the teacher provides resources that students will need to succeed at that task. In many cases, these resources will be informational—books, websites, videos, diagrams, and so on. In other cases, these resources might be more material—models or building materials.
Providing informational handouts	The teacher provides students with informational handouts that they can keep and refer back to if they have questions about a long-term project or cognitively complex task. For example, a list of frequently asked questions about specific types of cognitively complex tasks and their answers can help students independently resolve some confusion.
Teaching research skills	Teachers provide direct instruction in how to independently find resources and information that will help them complete cognitively complex tasks.
Conducting interviews	The teacher conducts interviews with students to keep track of their progress as they work on cognitively complex tasks and projects. The teacher might use a checklist or scoring scale to guide each interview and to help the students plan their next steps.
Circulating around the room	The teacher walks around the room while students work on cognitively complex tasks, allowing them to easily request assistance.
Collecting informal assessment information	The teacher examines students' responses on formative assessments of content related to their cognitively complex tasks to anticipate student needs and make helpful resources immediately available.
Offering feedback	The teacher offers feedback to students about their overall performance on cognitively complex tasks and makes specific suggestions regarding how students can complete their tasks.
Creating cognitive dissonance	The teacher seeks out information that does not align with students' hypotheses and presents that information to students to help them identify and correct errors in their thinking.

Source: Adapted from Marzano Resources, 2016dd.

Most of the strategies in table 5.2 address various ways of helping students be successful at their cognitively complex tasks. For example, providing resources involves teachers anticipating student needs as they progress through their tasks and being ready to address them at the right time with information, materials, or coaching. Teaching research skills involves direct instruction for those students who need help gathering information from various sources and analyzing results.

There is certainly no implied sequence to the strategies in table 5.2. As they observe students engaging in their complex tasks, teachers utilize those strategies that fit the needs of individual students, small groups, or the whole class.

When the strategies in this element produce the desired effects, teachers will observe the following behaviors in students.

- Students seek out the teacher for advice regarding their projects.
- Students can explain how the teacher's actions help them with their projects.
- Students are actively working on their complex tasks, making adaptations as they do so.

Element 14: Generating and Defending Claims

The ultimate purpose of engaging students in cognitively complex tasks is to provide opportunities for them to generate new conclusions and provide evidence for their conclusions. The specific strategies for this element appear in table 5.3.

Table 5.3: Generating and Defending Claims

Strategy	Description
Introducing the concept of claims and support	The teacher introduces the concept of claims and support to students. At first, it is enough to introduce the idea that a claim is simply something we believe to be true. Our reasons and evidence for our claims are referred to as support.
Presenting the formal structure of claims and support	When students are familiar with the general concept of claims and support, the teacher provides them with the more formal distinctions. Specifically, at a formal level, support for a claim should include grounds, backing, and qualifiers.
Generating claims	The teacher provides students with guidance in and opportunities to generate claims.
Providing grounds	The teacher has students state their claims with the word *because* at the end and then finish the sentence. The portion of the sentence following the because is grounds for the claim.
Providing backing	The teacher has students produce backing and helps students determine its type: expert opinion, research results, or factual information.
Generating qualifiers	The teacher helps students generate qualifiers by asking them to collect a wide range of evidence for a claim. Students sort that evidence into two categories: (1) evidence that supports the claim and (2) evidence that does not support the claim. Evidence supporting the claim is sorted into grounds (which are more general) and backing (which is more specific). Students can use evidence that does not support the claim to generate qualifiers.
Formally presenting claims	The teacher has students present claims formally, either orally or in writing. When done orally, this takes a significant amount of time but provides rich opportunities for students in class to ask questions and make comments to the presenter.

Source: Adapted from Marzano Resources, 2016p.

Many of the strategies in table 5.3 involve the basic components of a well-structured argument. For example, the strategy of generating claims involves teaching students about the nature of claims. This includes making the distinction between *claims* (which are statements of belief or opinion) and *facts* (which are statements that can be readily confirmed or denied). Well-structured arguments also involve grounds, backing, and qualifiers. *Grounds* represent the first line of evidence with a second tier of support referred to as *backing*. *Qualifiers* are statements that indicate the degree of certainty students have about their claims. Ultimately, these pieces all work together to form a cohesive whole. The teacher presents this overall structure to students in the strategy of presenting the formal structure of claims and support. Once students have this omnibus strategy under control, they can generate and defend claims in any context.

When the strategies in this element produce the desired effects, teachers will observe the following behaviors in students.

- Students can generate claims based on their cognitively complex tasks.
- Students can provide grounds.
- Students can provide backing for grounds.
- Students can provide qualifiers.
- Students can describe why generating and supporting claims helps them learn more deeply and rigorously.

Planning

The design question pertaining to implementing knowledge application lessons is, After presenting new content, how will I design and deliver lessons that help students generate and defend claims through knowledge application? The three elements that pertain to this design area provide specific guidance regarding this overall design question. Teachers can easily turn these elements into more focused planning questions.

- **Element 12:** How will I engage students in cognitively complex tasks?
- **Element 13:** How will I provide resources and guidance?
- **Element 14:** How will I help students generate and defend claims?

These specific planning questions can be thought of as sequential in nature. The first thing a teacher plans for is the cognitively complex task in which students will engage. Options here include the various types of tasks (experimental inquiry, problem solving, decision making, investigation, and invention). Options also include students selecting their own type of task. With cognitively complex tasks identified, the teacher identifies and gathers resources students might need and has them ready as she helps students engage in their projects. Finally, the teacher plans how students will generate and support claims. While this activity should always be an aspect of knowledge application tasks, there are some situations in which students should informally address claims and their support, and other situations in which students should address them with extended presentations. For example, if a unit is long enough, the teacher might plan for students to make formal presentations of their claims in written form with accompanying documentation. If the unit is short, the teacher might opt for students to present their claims orally in small groups without written documentation.

Implications for Change

As was the case with practicing and deepening lessons, an important implication for change regarding conducting knowledge application lessons is the need to directly teach skills other than academic content. The skills important to knowledge application lessons are cognitively complex tasks and claims. As before, these skills are all aspects of college and career readiness.

The quintessential skill within this set is generating and defending claims. I believe it should be a process that runs throughout the entire K–12 curriculum. Simple versions would be presented at the primary levels. At the secondary level, students would not only engage in more complex versions of the process but also delve deeply into the various types of evidence considered acceptable in different disciplines (such as statistical evidence, observational evidence, and evidence deduced from accepted principles). Operationally, every student should know the structure of well-known arguments since it spirals up throughout the curriculum. Figure 5.1 provides a graphic model of an argument's overall structure.

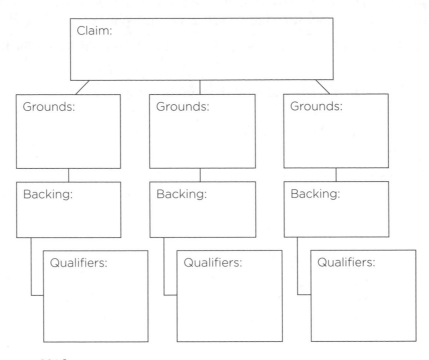

Source: Marzano Resources, 2016p.

Figure 5.1: The structure of an argument.

Of the components in figure 5.1, backing is the area of greatest need and provides the opportunity for the greatest change. This is because humans do not naturally go beyond grounds (Marzano & Marzano, 2015). Grounds are what we provide when someone asks, "Why do you think that is true?" These reasons require little thought. When we say that a particular movie was not good and someone asks why, we can easily provide answers: it was too long or too short; it was too complex. These reasons are right at the surface of our thinking. It is providing evidence that supports our reasons that makes us think at deeper levels. For example, being able to explain why a movie being too complex makes it a bad movie from our perspective involves a level of rigor teachers rarely ask students to demonstrate. This is unfortunate because this type of thinking is at the core of *effective learning*, or the gradual accumulation of an integrated set of concepts, generalizations, and principles that occurs through a disciplined execution of the process of argumentation.

CHAPTER 6

Using Strategies That Appear in All Types of Lessons

There are a number of strategies that commonly appear in all three types of lessons: (1) direct instruction lessons, (2) practicing and deepening lessons, and (3) knowledge application lessons.

> The desired mental states and processes
> common to these ubiquitous strategies are:
>
> Students continually integrate new knowledge with
> old knowledge and revise their understanding accordingly.

The elements that focus on this design area help students continually loop through content they are learning so that they might integrate new knowledge with old. The notion that students must cycle through and make changes in their existing knowledge base is certainly not new. For example, Jean Piaget (1971) distinguishes between the learning processes of assimilation and accommodation. *Assimilation* refers to the initial linking of new content to old content. New content is assimilated into existing knowledge structures. *Accommodation* occurs more gradually as existing knowledge becomes redesigned as a result of assimilation with new information. David E. Rumelhart and Donald A. Norman (1978) describe three types of knowledge change: (1) accretion, (2) tuning, and (3) restructuring. *Accretion* and *tuning* refer to additions to knowledge over time. Accretion happens relatively quickly. Tuning is more gradual and involves the expression of knowledge in more parsimonious forms. *Restructuring* is like Piaget's accommodation in that pre-existing knowledge structures are permanently redesigned as a function of the learning process. For example, a student might have a pre-existing knowledge structure for the relationship between the moon and tides, which involves only the distance between the Earth and the moon. However, after a set of particularly clear direct instruction lessons by the teacher, the student redesigns her knowledge structure adding variables like the tilt of the Earth and the gravitational pull of the sun. She also completely revamps the number and type of causal relationships among variables in her knowledge structure.

The following elements are important to strategies that appear in all types of lessons.

Element 15: Previewing Strategies

Previewing strategies provide students with a glimpse of the content that the teacher is about to address. Cognitively speaking, previewing strategies help activate students' prior knowledge. While such strategies are very common in direct instruction lessons, they are also applicable to practicing and deepening lessons as well as knowledge application lessons. Any time a significant amount of new content is presented, teachers are well advised to help activate students' prior knowledge. The specific strategies associated with this element appear in table 6.1.

Table 6.1: Previewing Strategies

Strategy	Description
Informational hooks	The teacher uses activities to stimulate interest in the lesson's content. These activities might include anecdotes; video clips; audio clips; newspaper headlines; and other short, attention-grabbing media to spark students' attention.
Bell ringers	As their name implies, bell ringers are activities at the very beginning of a class period that students are to engage in as soon as, or even before, the bell rings. For example, a teacher might have his or her students answer a brief question written on the board.
What do you think you know?	The teacher asks students to individually write down what they already know about an upcoming topic. After each student has created an individual list, the teacher asks students to pair up and discuss their previous knowledge and ideas. Finally, each pair shares its list, and the teacher creates a whole-class list of what students already know about upcoming content.
Overt linkages	The teacher helps students make overt links between content they have previously studied in class and new content by simply explaining the connections.
Preview questions	The teacher asks questions about upcoming content to pique students' curiosity and activate their prior knowledge.
Brief teacher summaries	The teacher provides students with an oral or written summary of content before presenting it. He or she also links upcoming content to past content.
Skimming	The teacher helps students skim written information on an upcoming topic by teaching them to look at major section headings and subheadings and asking them to analyze those headings to pick out main ideas and important concepts in the passage.
Teacher-prepared notes	The teacher provides an outline of the content to students before presenting it as new information.
K-W-L strategies	The teacher uses a K-W-L strategy before presenting new content. The letters of K-W-L stand for know, want to know, and learned.
Advance organizers	The teacher creates a visual representation or graphic organizer showing the structure and organization of new content and illustrating how new content connects to information previously learned in class.
Anticipation guides	Before presenting new content, the teacher has students respond to a series of statements that relate to upcoming information. After students respond to the statements, the teacher leads the class in a discussion about how students responded.
Word splashes	The teacher prepares a number of words and descriptions of those words associated with the new content and presents them to students. Students try to sort the terms into categories that make sense to them.
Preassessments	The teacher administers a preassessment to students before presenting new content. This assessment exposes students to the most important information in an upcoming presentation. The teacher can use preassessment results to gain an understanding of which students have a lot of prior knowledge about upcoming content and which do not.

Source: Adapted from Marzano Resources, 2016z.

Some of the strategies in table 6.1 are quite straightforward and can be done in a short amount of time. For example, overt linkages simply involve the teacher alerting students to the fact that new knowledge they are about to encounter is related to previous content they have experienced. For example, prior to watching a Khan Academy (www.khanacademy.org) illustration of the percolation process, the teacher might remind students that what they are about to see is identical to the last experiment they conducted, where soil acted as a filter as water sifted through it.

Other strategies in this set can extend over an entire class period. This is the case for the well-known strategy of K-W-L (*know*, *want to know*, and *learned*). At the beginning of a class, students identify what they think they know about the topic that is the lesson's focus. They also identify what they want to know. At the end of the lesson, they articulate what they learned. In addition to new knowledge, students might also identify the misconceptions they found in what they thought they knew at the beginning of class.

When the strategies in this element produce the desired effects, teachers will observe the following behaviors in students.

- Students can explain the links they are making with their prior knowledge.
- Students engage in brief summarizing activities.
- Students can make predictions about what they expect.

Element 16: Highlighting Critical Information

Highlighting critical information strategies involve the teacher pointing out what is important and what is less important in information he or she addresses in class. The need for these strategies stems from the fact that school bombards students with a myriad of incoming information even within the confines of a single class period. Students hear the teacher, and other students, talking about the content. They read about the content; they see pictures depicting the content and observe demonstrations. Not all of this information is equally important. The strategies within this element help students attend to the most important content. Highlighting critical information strategies appear in table 6.2.

Table 6.2: Highlighting Critical Information

Strategy	Description
Repeating the most important content	The teacher continually repeats information that is important to the lesson or unit when opportunities present themselves. Repeating not only identifies which information is critical but also helps students remember that information.
Asking questions that focus on critical information	The teacher asks questions that remind students of previous content and highlight what is important in the current content.
Using visual activities	The teacher uses storyboards, graphic organizers, and pictures to highlight critical information, help students create mental pictures of the information, and promote comprehension and recall.
Using narrative activities	The teacher uses stories to anchor information in memory and signal to students that certain information is important. The narrative structure of a story is also particularly useful for highlighting important relationships between different events or pieces of information.
Using tone of voice, gestures, and body position	The teacher uses tone of voice, gestures, and body position to emphasize important information.

continued →

Strategy	Description
Using pause time	The teacher pauses during the presentation of new content to highlight important points. The use of pause time when presenting information helps ensure that students have sufficient opportunity to take in and process content.
Identifying critical-input experiences	The teacher identifies those experiences that involve critical information. Critical-input experiences introduce important new content to students and are vital to enhancing student learning. The teacher takes special care in planning for these experiences.
Using explicit instruction to convey critical content	The teacher uses plain, clear language to identify and convey critical content and paces the delivery of content so that students have plenty of time to process the information.
Using dramatic instruction to convey critical content	The teacher asks students to participate in a dramatic activity that conveys the critical content. Dramatic activities can range from skits and role playing to hand gestures and other body movements.
Providing advance organizers to cue critical content	The teacher designs advance organizers that identify and preview critical content for students. Advance organizers can be anything from a simple verbal cue to a classroom chart to a descriptive metaphor for the content.
Using what students already know to cue critical content	The teacher uses what students already know to explain critical content. Specifically, the teacher provides students with a link to old knowledge for every critical aspect of new knowledge.

Source: Adapted from Marzano Resources, 2016q.

Some of the strategies in table 6.2 are quite subtle. Here the teacher draws attention to specific content by exaggerating his or her voice, gestures, and body position. For example, while reading a description of new information to students, the teacher might use more volume with information that is essential to understanding the topic. For gestures, the teacher might establish a signal like raising his or her hand in the air to indicate when something students are watching or listening to involves critical content. For body position, the teacher might move to a certain part of the room to signal that he or she is presenting critical content. Some strategies require extended time and structure. For example, consider dramatic instruction. Here the teacher develops a dramatic enactment for content that is critically important to a topic. For a lesson in a health class on specific refusal skills, the teacher might develop scenarios that students act out in class. There are eleven strategies in all for highlighting critical information, which allows teachers to accomplish the goal of focusing students on specific content without overusing any one strategy.

When the strategies in this element produce the desired effects, teachers will observe the following behaviors in students.

- Students can describe the level of importance of specific information.
- Students can explain why specific content is important to know.
- Students visibly adjust their level of attention when teachers present important content.

Element 17: Reviewing Content

Review strategies provide students with opportunities to revisit what they have previously learned. This builds in a loop that not only helps students recall content but also change their thinking. The specific strategies for this element appear in table 6.3.

Table 6.3: Reviewing Content

Strategy	Description
Cumulative review	The teacher not only reviews content from the current unit but helps students relate it to content from previous units. Cumulative review also involves students identifying and correcting misconceptions they held previously and creating new generalizations.
Cloze activity	The teacher presents students with information they previously learned with pieces missing and asks them to fill in the missing pieces.
Summary	To review previously learned content, the teacher has the class briefly discuss what information it remembers or finds important using short summaries. The teacher can either create summaries for students to review or ask students to prepare summaries as the basis of discussion.
Presented problem	The teacher presents students with a problem that requires them to use information they previously learned to solve that problem.
Demonstration	The teacher asks students to demonstrate a skill or process that requires them to use information or a procedure they previously learned.
Brief practice test or exercise	The teacher asks students to complete a test or exercise that prompts them to remember and apply information they previously learned. After the test or exercise, students review any information they remembered or applied incorrectly.
Questioning	The teacher asks questions that require students to recall, recognize, or apply information they previously learned. These questions might also require students to make inferences or decisions based on the information.
Give one, get one	After locating and writing information on a specific topic in their academic notebooks, the teacher has students stand up and move to find a partner, carrying their notebooks with them. The pair compares what each student has recorded in his or her academic notebook.

Source: Adapted from Marzano Resources, 2016ii.

Some of the strategies in table 6.3 are relatively indirect ways of reviewing content. For example, consider questioning as a review strategy. To review previously addressed content about the geometry concept of area, the teacher simply asks students to respond to two or three questions about the concept at the beginning of class. Some strategies are rather direct but relatively brief in duration. For example, the teacher designs summaries to capture important content he or she previously addressed. The teacher reads these at the beginning of class or gives them to the students to read. Still other strategies involve student cooperation. For example, the give one, get one strategy involves students working in pairs. Each pair shows its notes (typically recorded in a notebook) regarding a topic previously addressed. Each member gets some new insights by viewing his or her partner's notes and helps give new insights by sharing what he or she has written.

Cumulative review is the quintessential review technique. The technique has four steps.

1. After the first unit or set of lessons in a school year, students record key content.
2. After the next unit or set of related lessons, students record key content. In addition, students identify misconceptions about old content they are now aware of based on the new content they have learned. Students also create generalizations based on the new and old content.
3. Students repeat step two with each new unit or set of lessons.
4. Periodically, students list their generalizations from previous units or sets of lessons and create one or more all-encompassing generalizations.

Cumulative review is a robust strategy that, when executed throughout a school year, ensures that content is kept fresh in students' minds.

When the strategies in this element produce the desired effects, teachers will observe the following behaviors in students.

- Students can describe their previous understanding of content.
- Students are rethinking what they have previously learned.
- Students ask questions about what they have previously learned.

Element 18: Revising Knowledge

Revising knowledge strategies provide students with concrete opportunities to change, add to, and delete from what they have previously learned. This, of course, is at the core of what Piaget (1971) refers to as *accommodation*, and what Rumelhart and Norman (1981) refer to as *restructuring*.

Specific strategies for this element appear in table 6.4.

Table 6.4: Revising Knowledge

Strategy	Description
Academic notebook entries	The teacher asks students to make new entries in their academic notebooks after a critical-input experience, after group work or processing, or after reviewing and correcting homework. Over the course of a unit, and during related units, students re-examine their notebooks to correct inaccuracies or complete information.
Academic notebook review	The teacher has students use their academic notebooks to identify important vocabulary terms, big ideas and concepts, generalizations, and other information they should study for an exam or quiz.
Peer feedback	The teacher has students trade academic notebooks and respond in writing to each other's entries.
Assignment revision	The teacher provides feedback on assignments and returns them to students. The teacher offers students the opportunity to revise their assignments according to the feedback and resubmit it to try to obtain a higher score.
The five basic processes	The teacher directs students in using the five basic processes to revise their content knowledge: (1) reviewing prior understanding of the content, (2) identifying and correcting mistakes, (3) identifying gaps in knowledge and filling them in, (4) deciding where to amend prior knowledge, and (5) explaining the reasoning behind the revisions.
Visual symbols	The teacher directs students in the use of visual symbols to revise their content knowledge. Visual symbols are shorthand ways of highlighting information and changes in understanding when revising academic notes.
Writing tools	The teacher directs students to revise their knowledge through the use of writing tools. Writing tools involve activities such as summarizing, concluding, quick-writes, sentence stems, and student-generated assessments.

Source: Adapted from Marzano Resources, 2016jj.

As a set, the strategies in table 6.4 provide teachers with a wide variety of ways to facilitate students' thoughtful revision of their knowledge. For example, the strategy titled the five basic processes presents students with five steps for revision.

1. Review your knowledge.
2. Identify and correct any mistakes.
3. Identify and fill any gaps.
4. Decide where to amend prior knowledge.
5. Explain your reasons.

The strategy assignment revision is geared particularly to products students have developed. It includes the following components.

- Check for errors.
- Check for clarity.
- Check for organization.
- Check for thoroughness.

Academic notebook entries are the foundational strategy for revising knowledge. If academic notebooks are in place, students have a dynamic record of their initial understanding of topics and the changes in their understanding over time.

When the strategies in this element produce the desired effects, teachers will observe the following behaviors in students.

- Students make corrections in what they have previously learned.
- Students can explain previous misconceptions they had about the content.
- Students appear pleased with the increase in their understanding.

Element 19: Reflecting on Learning

Strategies for reflecting on learning not only focus students' attention on the content but also on themselves as learners. This renders their thinking highly metacognitive. The strategies for this element appear in table 6.5.

Table 6.5: Reflecting on Learning

Strategy	Description
Reflective journals	The teacher has students use a portion of their academic notebooks to respond to reflection questions. Questions might prompt students to reflect on what predictions they made about the day's lesson that were correct or incorrect, what information in the lesson was easy or difficult to understand, how well they understand the major material the class is studying, how well they think they did during the day, or what they think they could have done better during the day.
Think logs	The teacher asks students to reflect on specific cognitive skills (for example, classification, drawing inferences, decision making, creative thinking, or self-regulation) that the lesson emphasized.
Exit slips	At the end of a lesson, the teacher asks students to respond to specific reflective questions on an exit slip that they fill out before leaving the room. An exit slip's questions might include the following: What are the main ideas of today's lesson? What do you feel most and least sure about? Do you have specific questions about today's lesson? With which aspects of today's class work were you successful?
Knowledge comparisons	The teacher asks students to compare their current level of knowledge on a topic or level of competence with a procedure to their previous levels of knowledge or competence.
Two-column notes	The teacher has students use two-column notes as an extended reflection activity at the end of a lesson. In the left column, students record facts or other information that they found interesting from the lesson. In the right column, they record their reactions, questions, and extended ideas related to the facts or information in the left column.

Source: Adapted from Marzano Resources, 2016hh.

The implicit focus for the strategies in table 6.5 is to help students understand the learning process as one that requires their attention and effort. To illustrate, consider the strategy of exit slips. Teachers can use exit slips to ask questions about the content addressed in class, but they can also use them to ask questions like:

- "What could you do differently to improve your work?"
- "What could you do differently to improve your learning?"

Similarly, consider the strategy knowledge comparison. Here, students engage in a process in which they identify what new information they learned about a given topic and how they might improve their learning in the future.

When the strategies in this element produce the desired effects, teachers will observe the following behaviors in students.

- Students can describe what they are clear about and what they are confused about.
- Students can describe their levels of effort and the relationship of their effort to their learning.
- Students can describe what they might do to improve their learning.

Element 20: Assigning Purposeful Homework

Homework is perhaps one of the most misused strategies in K–12 classrooms; it is too often assigned as a matter of routine (see Marzano & Pickering, 2007a, 2007b, 2007c). As the title of this element suggests, teachers must assign homework purposefully, which means they use it only when needed. The strategies for this element appear in table 6.6.

Table 6.6: Assigning Purposeful Homework

Strategy	Description
Homework preview	The teacher asks students to read a passage of text or view media that introduces a concept or idea they will study in class.
Homework to deepen knowledge	The teacher asks students to complete an assignment that helps them compare, contrast, or classify specific aspects of the content.
Homework to practice a process or skill	The teacher asks students who have demonstrated the ability to independently perform a process or skill in class to practice that process or skill independently to increase their fluency, speed, and accuracy with the process or skill.
Parent-assessed homework	The teacher provides specific directions to parents regarding homework. To assist students with homework, parents or family members ask reflective questions or listen to students give an oral summary of material they read. To help students develop fluency with skills or procedures, parents might also time them in executing a specific skill or process.

Source: Adapted from Marzano Resources, 2016ff.

Teachers can and should use homework as a form of previewing. For example, a useful homework assignment has students read a few pages in a textbook on the topic of magnetic forces the night before the teacher introduces the topic in class. Of course, students could access such information electronically, assuming that all students have access to the Internet at home. Other legitimate uses of homework include activities that help deepen students' knowledge and practice skills and processes. One important thing to consider when assigning homework is setting up specific guidelines regarding how parents might help. Parental help that facilitates the learning process includes asking students to summarize what they have learned from the homework and reflecting on their level of effort.

When the strategies in this element produce the desired effects, teachers will observe the following behaviors in students.

- Students understand the purpose of homework.
- Students are better prepared for new learning after being assigned homework.
- Students' understanding is deepened after being assigned homework.
- Students' speed, accuracy, or fluency is increased after being assigned homework.
- Students report that completing homework has helped them learn.

Element 21: Elaborating on Information

Elaboration is the process of going beyond what is initially learned. Elaboration strategies typically involve inferences that questions cue. The strategies for this element appear in table 6.7.

Table 6.7: Elaborating on Information

Strategy	Description
General inferential questions	The teacher uses two kinds of general inferential questions: (1) default and (2) reasoned inference. Default questions ask students to use their background knowledge to answer questions. Reasoned inference questions require students to provide reasons that logically lead to specific answers.
Elaborative interrogation	The teacher probes a student's answer by asking elaborative questions that prompt the student to reflect on the nature of and justifications for his or her response. The teacher asks, "Why do you believe that to be true?" in order to stimulate a student to provide evidence supporting his or her conclusion.
Questioning sequences	The teacher asks a sequence of detail, category, elaboration, and evidence questions to promote deep understanding and cognition. Detail questions identify and build a base of factual information that students can subsequently use to answer deeper, more complex questions. Category questions prompt students to generate lists of examples and identify a category's important characteristics. Elaboration questions encourage students to use these lists to form claims and conclusions. Evidence questions engage students in argumentation and evaluation as they find evidence to support their claims and revise their conclusions to exclude misconceptions or errors in reasoning.

Source: Adapted from Marzano Resources, 2016j.

Of the strategies in table 6.7, questioning sequences is the most robust. It requires that the teacher plan for four types of questions: (1) detail questions, (2) category questions, (3) elaboration questions, and (4) evidence questions. This sequential process ensures that students move from answering questions that are factually based to making inferences about the category to which a topic belongs and to generating and defending inferences.

When the strategies in this element produce the desired effects, teachers will observe the following behaviors in students.

- Students volunteer answers to inferential questions.
- Students provide explanations for their answers.
- Students describe the teacher's questions as challenging but helpful.

Element 22: Organizing Students to Interact

The final element that pertains to all types of lessons involves strategies for organizing students to interact in thoughtful ways that facilitate collaboration. Student interaction, when organized and executed properly, can enhance the impact of all elements in this chapter. The specific strategies for this element appear in table 6.8 (page 62).

Table 6.8: Organizing Students to Interact

Strategy	Description
Group for active processing	The teacher assigns students to groups of two to five members for processing new information. Assignments can be for a specific purpose (ad hoc groups) or long-term partnerships. In either case, groups should have operating rules of behavior and interaction.
Group norms creation	To ensure that student groups (especially long-term groups) function smoothly, the teacher asks students to create a list of norms (collective attitudes and behaviors) to govern the group's functioning.
Fishbowl demonstration	The teacher has her students form a circle ("fishbowl") around a group that demonstrates what effective group work looks like. The demonstration group might model behaviors such as paraphrasing, pausing, clarifying, questioning, brainstorming, and using respectful language.
Job cards	The teacher uses job cards to designate specific roles that students take within their groups. Jobs include facilitator, summarizer, questioner, and note taker.
Predetermined buddies to help form ad hoc groups	The teacher gives students a blank chart showing a clock (with twelve blanks, one for each hour), the seasons (with four blanks), or another theme-based graphic with blanks. Students find a partner for each blank and fill the partner's name in on their chart. When the teacher wants to form quick, ad hoc groups, he or she asks students to find their summer (or, for example, "two o'clock") buddies and students quickly pair up.
Contingency plan for ungrouped students	The teacher designates a meeting spot for students who don't have a group and can then help those students pair up or join existing groups. This helps avoid some students being left ungrouped when groups are student selected.
Group using preassessment information	After administering a preassessment, the teacher uses the information gained about individual students' prior knowledge to assign students to groups. In some cases, the teacher might want to mix students with high prior knowledge and students with low prior knowledge.
Pair-check	Within groups of four, students form pairs (two pairs per group) and designate who will be partner A and who will be partner B. Using a set of exercises, problems, or questions, partner A works on the first exercise, problem, or question while partner B coaches when necessary and praises partner A's work when complete. Pairs then switch roles.
Think-pair-share and think-pair-square	After grouping students in pairs, the teacher presents a problem. Students think about the problem individually for a predetermined amount of time. Then, students each share their thoughts. Pairs discuss and come to a consensus about their solution. The teacher then asks pairs to share what they decided with the class.
Student tournaments	The teacher organizes students into teams that then compete in various academic games. Team members are remixed after each unit to ensure that students have the opportunity to work with a variety of other students.
Inside-outside circle	The teacher has students form two concentric circles with an equal number of students in each circle. Students forming the inner circle stand facing outward, and students forming the outward circle stand facing inward. The teacher asks a question or presents a problem, and students discuss their thoughts, answers, and solutions with the person facing them. The circle rotates so that pairs are mixed.
Cooperative learning	The teacher structures and governs the use of cooperative learning during cognitively complex tasks. This involves (1) designing structures for group and individual accountability, (2) providing ongoing coaching of students, (3) specifying clear roles and responsibilities for all group members, and (4) using a variety of grouping criteria and grouping structures.
Peer-response groups	The teacher has students work with peers to give and receive feedback on complex tasks. The teacher assigns roles to students and uses scoring scales or checklists to ensure similar standards for each group member.
Peer tutoring	The teacher invites advanced students to volunteer to help students who need just a little assistance to move up to the next level.

Strategy	Description
Structured grouping	The teacher designs and implements structured group activities that feature both individual and group accountability. Individual group members carry out specific tasks and responsibilities while working together on the final product. Structured group activities deepen and extend students' understanding of a topic.
Group reflecting on learning	The teacher organizes students into groups to reflect on their learning progress. The structure of the reflection process guides students in sharing their reflections, encouraging each other, and identifying ways to grow in their learning.

Source: Adapted from Marzano Resources, 2016w.

The strategies in table 6.8 represent a broad array of ways teachers can organize students and guide them to interact. They all have somewhat different emphases; consequently, a teacher must determine which interaction strategy is most appropriate for the type of lesson and content. For example, peer tutoring works well with direct instruction lessons regarding declarative knowledge. A central feature of peer tutoring is to match students who understand the content well with students who are struggling. If a direct instruction lesson is intended to introduce content regarding the topic of a market economy, the teacher plans peer tutoring in such a way that students who grasp the concept are working with students who are struggling with it. Predetermined buddies for ad hoc groups works well with practicing and deepening lessons. This strategy provides groupings of students that teachers can employ at a moment's notice. If a teacher has students engaged in a knowledge deepening activity that involves comparing the geometric processes of flips and slides, the teacher could quickly organize students into groups to compare their reactions to the activity.

When the strategies in this element produce the desired effects, teachers will observe the following behaviors in students.

- Students move into groups quickly and with purpose.
- Students treat each other with respect.
- Students interact in a manner that deepens their understanding.
- Students work efficiently in groups.

Planning

The design question pertaining to using strategies that appear in all types of lessons is, Throughout all types of lessons, what strategies will I use to help students continually integrate new knowledge with old knowledge and revise their understanding accordingly? The eight elements that pertain to this design area provide specific guidance regarding this overall design question. Teachers can easily turn these elements into more focused planning questions.

- **Element 15:** How will I help students preview content?
- **Element 16:** How will I highlight critical information?
- **Element 17:** How will I help students review content?
- **Element 18:** How will I help students revise knowledge?
- **Element 19:** How will I help students reflect on their learning?
- **Element 20:** How will I use purposeful homework?
- **Element 21:** How will I help students elaborate on information?
- **Element 22:** How will I organize students to interact?

Planning for this design question requires a balance across elements. Theoretically, a teacher could use every element discussed in this chapter in every direct instruction lesson, every practicing and deepening lesson, and every knowledge application lesson, but this would not be wise practice. This is not to say that some strategies shouldn't appear in every lesson. Indeed, highlighting critical information and some forms of elaborating and reviewing should probably appear in every type of lesson. Teachers sometimes use other elements with specific lesson types. For example, teachers most commonly use previewing in direct instruction lessons. Organizing strategies can easily appear in all types of lessons, but time should also be set aside for students to work independently. Elements can be staggered. For example, a teacher can use revising strategies one day and reflection strategies another.

Implications for Change

The major change the strategies in this design area imply is that educators should view learning as a constructive process in which students constantly update their knowledge. This requires iterative and multiple exposures to the content. At the classroom level, this means that teachers must seek out and honor the revisions students make in their knowledge. This does not involve blind acceptance of anything a student says. Rather, teachers should constantly ask students to articulate the reasoning underlying the changes students have made in their thinking.

For example, a teacher might notice that a particular student's revision in his academic notebook still contains some errors. The teacher asks the student to explain his thinking. Instead of correcting the student's errors, the teacher ends the conversation by saying, "You've done some good thinking here and are getting closer. But there are still a few things you should consider in more depth." The teacher then points out specific topics for the student to attend to.

When teachers execute it properly, this type of interaction is a cultural shift in the classroom and should be immediately apparent in the level and type of discourse observable in the classroom (Cazden, 1986). For example, a classroom designed to have students continually integrate new knowledge with old knowledge and revise their understanding accordingly exhibits a great deal of student dialogue with peers and with the teacher. The most salient dynamic of this type of interaction is the continual resurrection of topics from past units and lessons to inform topics from new lessons and units. Discussions focus on how previous conceptions have changed and how new questions have arisen.

I believe that the dynamic of integrating new knowledge with old knowledge and revising understanding accordingly is almost nonexistent as a formal aspect of K–12 instruction. Instead, teachers typically move through content with little time or resources to continually make additions and corrections to old content while processing new content. Emphasis on this design area might generate huge benefits in enhanced student learning.

CHAPTER 7

Using Engagement Strategies

As described in the introduction, the broad category of context refers to students' mental readiness during the teaching-learning process. Specifically, for students to be ready to learn, they must have their needs met relative to engagement, order, a sense of belonging, and a sense of high expectations.

Engagement is possibly the gatekeeper to mental readiness. It is certainly a common term in education but educators lack clear agreement of its meaning (Marzano & Pickering, 2011). *The New Art and Science of Teaching* addresses this issue through the lens of desired mental states and processes.

> The desired mental states and processes for strategies related to engagement are:
>
> Students are paying attention, energized, intrigued, and inspired.

Engagement is divided into four components: (1) paying attention, (2) being energized, (3) being intrigued, and (4) being inspired.

The following elements are important to fostering this broad perspective on engagement.

Element 23: Noticing and Reacting When Students Are Not Engaged

The most basic set of strategies that relate to engagement simply involve a teacher being aware of and reacting when students are disengaged. If a teacher does not have this awareness and execute appropriate strategies, he or she will probably not keep students engaged at any level. Executing this element can take many forms. Strategies for this element appear in table 7.1 (page 66).

Table 7.1: Noticing and Reacting When Students Are Not Engaged

Strategy	Description
Monitoring individual student engagement	The teacher scans the room and identifies specific students who appear to be disengaged to ensure high levels of classroom engagement. The teacher engages in this type of monitoring during small-group instruction as well as during individual seatwork.
Monitoring overall class engagement	The teacher monitors levels of engagement of the whole class. When monitoring class engagement, a teacher assesses the degree to which the class seems to be interested in the work at hand without focusing on specific students.
Using self-reported student engagement data	The teacher periodically asks students to signal their level of engagement. The teacher might ask students to self-report their engagement levels informally by asking students to raise their hands if they feel their energy levels dropping or create a system to let students consistently report their engagement.
Re-engaging individual students	Once a teacher identifies a student who is not engaged or reacting to the content he or she is presenting, the teacher takes action to re-engage that specific student.
Boosting overall class energy levels	If a teacher notices that the energy levels in the classroom as a whole are low, the teacher ceases instruction and announces that something must be done to increase everyone's engagement. The teacher invites students to provide suggestions.

Source: Adapted from Marzano Resources, 2016v.

The strategies in table 7.1 focus on a simple dynamic. The teacher monitors the students' engagement levels. If engagement is waning, the teacher does something about it. Some of the strategies simply involve enhancing teachers' awareness. For example, monitoring overall class engagement involves periodically taking stock of students' attention levels as a whole. Other strategies require students to signal their level of engagement. For example, using student self-reported data involves students providing teachers with some overt cue indicating how engaged they are, perhaps using color-coded cards indicating levels of engagement. Some strategies like boosting overall class energy levels are very general in nature. Others, like re-engaging individual students, are highly focused.

When the strategies in this element produce the desired effects, teachers will observe the following behaviors in students.

- Students appear aware of the fact that the teacher is taking note of their engagement levels.
- Students try to increase their engagement levels when appropriate.
- When asked, students explain that the teacher expects high engagement levels.

Element 24: Increasing Response Rates

Increasing response rates enhances students' attention levels. *Response rates* refer to how many students are responding to the teacher's questions and queries. On the surface, asking questions of students might seem like a fail-safe engagement strategy—when students are answering questions, they are obviously paying attention to what is occurring in class. However, from a whole-class perspective, asking questions can be highly disengaging, especially if one student only is providing an answer to a specific question. While the single student who has been called on is attending to the question, no one else has to. The strategies within this element are geared toward getting as many students as possible to answer any given question. Strategies for this element appear in table 7.2.

Table 7.2: Increasing Response Rates

Strategy	Description
Random names	The teacher writes each student's name on a separate slip of paper or popsicle stick and keeps it in a container. After asking a question, the teacher selects a name at random from the jar and calls on that student to answer.
Hand signals	The teacher has students respond nonverbally to a question that has a limited number of possible responses. For example, students use a thumbs-up, thumbs-down, or thumbs-sideways to indicate their levels of understanding regarding content the teacher is addressing.
Response cards	The teacher asks students to write their answers on small (for example, 12 × 12 inch) whiteboards or chalkboards and reveal them to the teacher simultaneously.
Response chaining	After a student responds to a question, the teacher asks a second student to explain why the initial student's answer was correct, partially correct, or incorrect. The teacher can repeat the process for the second student's response.
Paired response	Students confer in pairs to answer a question. The teacher then calls on a pair. One student verbalizes the answer for the pair, or both can contribute.
Choral response	The teacher presents critical information in a clear and concise statement and asks the class to repeat the information as a group. The goal is to form an "imprint" of important information.
Wait time	The teacher pauses for at least three seconds after posing a question. The teacher also pauses for three seconds between student answers.
Elaborative interrogation	After a student answers a question, the teacher probes the answer by asking, "How do you know that to be true?" or "Why is that so?"
Multiple types of questions	The teacher uses a combination of types of questions such as retrieval questions (these require students to recognize, recall, and execute knowledge that was directly taught), analytical questions (these require students to take information apart and determine how the parts relate to the whole), predictive questions (these require students to form conjectures and hypotheses about what will happen next in a narrative or sequence of information or actions), interpretive questions (these require students to make and defend inferences about the intentions of an author), and evaluative questions (these require students to use criteria to make judgments and assessments of something).

Source: Adapted from Marzano Resources, 2016r.

Some of the strategies in table 7.2 allow all students to respond to a single question. For example, response cards involve all students in class writing their answer on small, handheld whiteboards and showing their answers to the teacher. All students are responding, therefore, all students are paying attention. Some strategies are rather short term in their effect. For example, wait time involves a teacher pausing for a few seconds between the time she asks a question and calls on a student to answer. For the few moments the teacher is waiting to call on someone, all students are probably attending to the question. Some strategies, like response chaining, require students to attend to other students' answers since the teacher will expect students to agree or disagree with the initial student's answer and explain why.

When the strategies in this element produce the desired effects, teachers will observe the following behaviors in students.

- Multiple students respond or the entire class responds to questions.
- Students pay attention to the answers other students provide.
- Students can describe the thinking that led to specific answers.
- Students are aware that the teacher expects all students to answer questions.

Element 25: Using Physical Movement

Physical movement strategies have a direct connection to students' energy levels. This makes sense intuitively—movement is obviously related to increased energy. It also makes sense physiologically—movement increases blood flow to the brain which stimulates engagement (Marzano & Pickering, 2011). The strategies for this element appear in table 7.3.

Table 7.3: Using Physical Movement

Strategy	Description
Stand up and stretch	Periodically, the teacher asks students to stand up and stretch. This is especially useful when students need to change focus or their concentration level.
Vote with your feet	The teacher posts signs in specific parts of the room identifying responses to a true-or-false or multiple-choice question or reactions to answers to a question (incorrect, partially correct, or totally correct). Students move to the location that has the sign with the answer they think is correct.
Corners activities	The teacher splits the class into four groups, which then rotate to each of the four corners of the classroom to examine four different questions related to key content. The teacher assigns a recorder to stay in each corner to summarize students' comments about that corner's question.
Stand and be counted	The teacher presents a self-assessment scale, gives students a moment to think, and then prompts students at each level of the scale to stand. For example, a teacher might present a 1–4 scale in which 1 indicates "I didn't understand any of the concepts presented in this lesson" and 4 indicates "I clearly understand all the concepts presented in this lesson."
Body representations	The teacher asks students to create body representations in which they act out important content or critical aspects of a topic (for example, forming cause-and-effect chains, physically acting out key sequence elements, or representing vocabulary terms).
Drama-related activities	The teacher asks students to act out an event they are studying, taking the roles of various participants in the event.

Source: Adapted from Marzano Resources, 2016pp.

Some of the strategies in table 7.3 incorporate physical movement into activities that basically help students process content. For example, corners activities require students to rotate through the four corners of the classroom. While at each corner, they learn and discuss information relative to the overall topic the teacher is addressing. Some strategies are basically response rate strategies that include movement. For example, the stand-and-be-counted strategy has students stand up if their self-assessed understanding of a topic is at a specific level on a teacher-provided scale. Some strategies use physical movement to help students create representations of the content. For example, dramatic activities require students to act out the critical aspects of content that the class has addressed.

When the strategies in this element produce the desired effects, teachers will observe the following behaviors in students.

- Students actively engage in the strategies.
- Students' energy levels appear to increase.
- Students can explain how the physical movement keeps their interest and helps them learn.

Element 26: Maintaining a Lively Pace

The strategies within this element focus on students' energy levels, but they don't focus on things the teacher asks students to do. Instead, they involve actions the teacher takes that have an indirect effect on students' energy levels. The strategies for this element appear in table 7.4.

Table 7.4: Maintaining a Lively Pace

Strategy	Description
Instructional segments	The teacher ensures that each of the following aspects of management and instruction is well planned and occurs in a brisk, but unhurried, fashion: administrative tasks, presentation of new content, act of practicing and deepening understanding key knowledge and skills, application of knowledge to new situations, group organization, seatwork, and transitions.
Pace modulation	The teacher speeds up or slows down the pace of the lesson to meet the students' engagement needs.
Parking lot	If the teacher or students get stuck or bogged down on the answer to a specific question or issue, the teacher writes the problem in a space on the board called the parking lot. The teacher and students come back to the issue the next day after everyone has had time to think and gather information about it.
Motivational hooks	The teacher uses anecdotes, video clips, audio clips, newspaper headlines, and other short attention-grabbing media to spark students' attention.

Source: Adapted from Marzano Resources, 2016t.

The strategies in table 7.4 address a wide range of teacher actions and decisions. For example, the instructional segment strategy relates to effective preparation for the different types of activities that occur in the class. These include administrative tasks, seatwork, transitions, and the like. The more organized a teacher is for these types of activities, the more his or her class will run smoothly and quickly, thus decreasing the amount of downtime in the classroom.

Pace modulation refers to speeding up or slowing down depending on students' needs. Sometimes the teacher slows down the pace to emphasize content. Sometimes the teacher moves quickly through content because it is highly familiar to students. The changes in pace help keep students energized.

The parking lot strategy allows students to post questions or concerns about a topic that the teacher goes back to at the end of class or the next day and addresses thoroughly. This strategy ensures that the pace of the class stays lively but does not result in individual student's questions being ignored.

Motivational hooks are just what their name implies. They are quickly presented pieces of content that are highly interesting and help capture and maintain student interest.

When the strategies in this element produce the desired effects, teachers will observe the following behaviors in students.

- Students quickly adapt to changes in classroom activities and reengage in the content.
- Students report that the pace of the class is neither too fast nor too slow.

Element 27: Demonstrating Intensity and Enthusiasm

The strategies in this element relate most strongly to students' sense of intrigue about or interest in the content. Again, this deals more with teacher actions than with students' expected actions. If the teacher demonstrates intensity and enthusiasm about the content, students are more likely to perceive the content as intriguing and interesting. The strategies for this element appear in table 7.5.

Table 7.5: Demonstrating Intensity and Enthusiasm

Strategy	Description
Direct statements about the importance of content	To help students understand why they're learning the content, the teacher incorporates direct statements about the importance of specific content into the lesson.
Explicit connections	The teacher draws explicit connections between content and the world outside school in order to make the content more exciting or relevant for students.
Nonlinguistic representations	Nonlinguistic representations commonly take the form of graphic organizers, pictographs, flow charts, or diagrams. A teacher can use these visual elements to increase students' interest in the material and help them visualize connections or patterns in the content they might not have recognized previously.
Personal stories	The teacher tells personal stories about the content to make it more accessible to students. The teacher might recall and retell his or her own reactions to the content, identify content that was difficult to understand at first, or explain why content provided important personal insights.
Verbal and nonverbal signals	The teacher uses verbal signals such as the volume and tone of voice, verbal emphasis on specific words or phrases, pauses to build anticipation and excitement, and the rate of speech to communicate intensity and enthusiasm to students.
Humor	Depending on a teacher's personality and instructional style, he or she might show a funny political cartoon or video, direct jokes at him- or herself, use silly quotes or voices, or point out absurdities in a textbook, film, or article to demonstrate enthusiasm for a topic.
Quotations	The teacher uses quotations to add context to the content he or she is presenting. For quotations that are relevant to content, teachers might search for quotations by relevant historical figures or about the topic being taught.
Movie and film clips	The teacher uses video clips of movies, documentaries, and news stories to help students gain new perspectives on content and connect content to real-world events and situations.

Source: Adapted from Marzano Resources, 2016f.

Some of the strategies in table 7.5 relate to rather subtle teacher behaviors. For example, verbal and non-verbal indicators of enthusiasm include variation of speed and tone, pausing to build anticipation, smiling, direct eye contact with students, clapping, thumbs-up, and high-fives. All of these send the message that the teacher is enthusiastic about the content.

Other teacher strategies are more direct and concrete. For example, personal stories are anecdotes a teacher offers about his or her involvement with the content. These stories might come up spontaneously as the teacher recalls his or her first interactions with the content.

Some strategies require overt preparation and research. For example, teachers can identify historical stories and quotations related to the content to communicate its value. Teachers execute some strategies, like humor, more spontaneously.

When the strategies in this element produce the desired effects, teachers will observe the following behaviors in students.

- Students say the teacher likes the content and likes teaching.
- Students' attention levels increase in response to the teacher's interest and enthusiasm.

Element 28: Presenting Unusual Information

The strategies in this element all serve to stimulate students' sense of intrigue about content. Unusual information almost always stimulates intrigue. This is because the human mind organizes knowledge in relatively neat, well-contained packets. When we experience or learn something that does not fit into one of our preordained packets, we become intrigued (Marzano & Pickering, 2011). Such is the power of unusual information—by definition, it is out of the ordinary relative to what we know about something or someone. The strategies for this element appear in table 7.6.

Table 7.6: Presenting Unusual Information

Strategy	Description
Teacher-presented information	The teacher presents unusual or intriguing information to capture students' attention. Facts related to the content are preferable, but any unusual information can attract students' attention.
Webquests	The teacher has students explore the Internet and find a range of obscure but interesting facts and ideas associated with the content they are studying.
Fast facts	The teacher asks students to share the most unusual (but factual) information they have discovered about a particular topic. To use this strategy, the teacher must provide time for students to research information about the topic they are addressing.
Believe it or not	The teacher helps students create an electronic database of unusual or little-known information about the content they are studying. This can extend from one year to the next, with each class reading previous class contributions, correcting misconceptions where appropriate, and adding their own unusual information.
History files	The teacher has students research different historical perceptions regarding the content areas they are studying.
Guest speakers and first-hand consultants	The teacher has guests share experiences from their careers that relate to the content.

Source: Adapted from Marzano Resources, 2016y.

Some of the strategies in table 7.6 require the teacher to generate unusual information. For example, in the teacher-presented information strategy, the teacher uses a variety of sources to identify interesting facts that relate to the content the class is addressing. During a unit on Ernest Hemingway, for example, a teacher might look up biographical information about the famous writer and collect a few intriguing facts, such as his parents dressing him as a girl during his early years of life. The teacher presents such facts and discusses them with students. Other strategies require the students to generate unusual information. For example, in the fast facts strategy, students find and share intriguing information. They might do this on the spot with time during class to look up interesting facts that pertain to the content. Still other strategies involve community members. For example, in the guest speakers or first-hand consultants strategy, the teacher seeks out local speakers who can add unusual information about the content. During the unit on Hemingway, the teacher might ask a local graduate student doing his or her master's thesis on Hemingway to come in and address the class.

When the strategies in this element produce the desired effects, teachers will observe the following behaviors in students.

- Student engagement levels increase with the presentation of unusual information.
- Students can explain how the unusual information makes the content more interesting.
- Students ask questions about the unusual information that is presented.

Element 29: Using Friendly Controversy

Strategies within this element stimulate intrigue and interest in students. This is a natural by-product of controversy. When we are disagreeing with someone, we are usually highly engaged. However, controversy can become so emotionally charged that the participants become combative. When this occurs, controversy adds little or nothing useful to an individual's knowledge base. When individuals conduct controversy in a civil manner, it can enhance the subject-matter knowledge and the self-knowledge of all concerned—hence the term *friendly controversy*. The strategies for this element appear in table 7.7.

Table 7.7: Using Friendly Controversy

Strategy	Description
Friendly controversy	The teacher has students explain and defend their positions on topics about which they disagree. The teacher asks students to follow specific guidelines when engaging in friendly controversy. Guidelines ensure that students feel free to disagree with others but do so respectfully and allow for everyone to express their opinions.
Class vote	The teacher has students vote on a particular issue. Before and after the vote, students discuss the merits of various positions. The teacher might ask students to vote again after the final discussion.
Seminars	The teacher organizes students into groups and has them explore a text, video, or other resource that expresses highly opinionated perspectives about a key issue or topic related to the curriculum content. After discussion in small groups, the whole class joins together to discuss. All groups might explore the same resource or each group might investigate a different perspective on the same topic.
Expert opinions	The teacher has students research expert opinions on contrasting perspectives and points of view about a particular issue or topic. The class then discusses the merits of the various perspectives and the validity (or lack thereof) of a particular thinker's ideas, positions, and evidence.
Opposite point of view	The teacher has students defend the opposite point of view from the one they agree with or support.
Diagrams comparing perspectives	The teacher has students use a Venn diagram to compare various points of view. The diagram might highlight areas of congruence and areas of disagreement between two or three ideas.
Lincoln-Douglas debate	The teacher chooses two teams to debate opposing sides of a specific policy or issue. One side argues in favor of the policy or issue (affirmative team) and the other side argues against it (negative team). Each side gets the opportunity to make an opening argument, cross-examine the opposing side, and present a rebuttal.
Town-hall meeting	The teacher facilitates a discussion among several parties with varying perspectives, as might be seen in a local town-hall meeting.
Legal model	The teacher has students critically examine how U.S. Supreme Court decisions affect policy as they form their opinions and arguments based on textual evidence from past Supreme Court cases.

Source: Adapted from Marzano Resources, 2016oo.

Teachers can execute some of the strategies in table 7.7 in a relatively short period of time. For example, teachers can do a class vote with very little planning. The teacher raises an issue that students seem to have differing opinions on, and the teacher calls for a class vote after parsing the issue into two or more differing positions. Students then vote for the position they most agree with. To add some movement, the teacher might ask the students to stand and walk to different parts of the room that represent a given position. Students for a given position then defend their choice.

Other strategies require a significant amount of preparation. For example, the Lincoln-Douglas debate model has a specific structure that requires preparation to execute well. It includes an opening argument, a cross-examination, and a rebuttal. The teacher usually executes this strategy using teams with participants having adequate time to prepare.

When the strategies in this element produce the desired effects, teachers will observe the following behaviors in students.

- Students readily engage in the friendly controversy activities.
- Students describe friendly controversy activities as *stimulating*, *fun*, and *interesting*.
- Students can explain how the friendly controversy activities help them better understand the content.

Element 30: Using Academic Games

To most students, games are intrinsically engaging. They intrigue students by their very structure. Specifically, all games require a search for something that is missing or unknown but circumstances provide clues as to how to complete the scenario (Marzano & Pickering, 2011). For example, the popular game *Pictionary* works on this principle. A word or phrase represents the unknown content. A contestant's pictures represent the clues that players use to determine what is unknown. The strategies for this element appear in table 7.8.

Table 7.8: Using Academic Games

Strategy	Description
What Is the Question?	The teacher creates and displays a matrix with content-based categories across the top and point categories (generally 100, 200, 300, 400, and 500) down the side. The teacher also creates clues (words, pictures, or a combination of the two) in each matrix cell, with more difficult clues corresponding to higher point values.
Name That Category	The teacher creates a game board that looks like a pyramid divided into sections with various categories and point values. The teacher organizes students into teams with one clue giver and one or more guessers. Teams sit so that clue givers face the game board and guessers face the opposite direction. The teacher reveals one category on the game board at a time. Teams compete to determine who answers all questions in the pyramid first.
Talk a Mile a Minute	The teacher prepares a set of cards, each with a category and list of items that fit in that category. The teacher organizes students into teams and each team designates one team member as the talker. The teacher gives a card to each talker. The talker tries to get his or her team to say each of the words on the card by quickly describing them.
Classroom Feud	The teacher constructs at least one question for every student in the class. Questions can be multiple choice, fill in the blank, or short answer. The teacher organizes students into teams, and they take turns being the responder for their team. The teacher presents a question to a responder who has fifteen seconds to confer with team members and identify the team's answer. The responder tells the team's answer to the teacher.
Which One Doesn't Belong?	The teacher creates word groups containing three terms that are similar and one term that is different. The teacher displays one word group at a time. Students, working independently or in groups, have a set amount of time to pick out the term that does not belong and write down why they think that term is different.
Inconsequential competition	The teacher uses any type of inconsequential competition (including academic games like those previously described) to increase student engagement. While teams compete, it is only for fun. There are no formal positive or negative consequences associated with winning or losing.
Questions into games	The teacher turns questions into impromptu games by forming students into four equally sized groups before asking a series of questions during a lesson. After the teacher asks a question, group members talk together for one minute and record their answer on a response card. On the teacher's signal, each group holds up its answer.
Vocabulary review games	The teacher uses games to review vocabulary with students.

Source: Adapted from Marzano Resources, 2016nn.

While the games in table 7.8 are inherently engaging, teachers must gear them toward specific content if they are to enhance students' learning. For example, the game What Is the Question? is modeled after the popular television game show *Jeopardy!*. While the game-show version focuses on general knowledge usually involving trivia, the classroom version should always focus on the content from the current unit or previous units. Thus, games become a powerful form of review activity.

When the strategies in this element produce the desired effects, teachers will observe the following behaviors in students.

- Students engage in the academic games enthusiastically.
- Students can describe the content the games focus on.
- Students can explain how the games enhanced their understanding of the content.

Element 31: Providing Opportunities for Students to Talk About Themselves

When students are involved in activities that allow them to talk about themselves, they perceive that they are welcome in the class. Students talking about themselves can also be inspirational, at least in two ways. First, students might hear stories from their peers that inspire them to do things they would not have considered otherwise. Also, when communicating about themselves to others, students might develop better self-images simply by their willingness to share things they believe in. The strategies for this element appear in table 7.9.

Table 7.9: Providing Opportunities for Students to Talk About Themselves

Strategy	Description
Interest surveys	At the beginning of the school year or unit, the teacher administers an interest survey. Such surveys can cover a range of topics such as goals, personal or family history, existing knowledge about the content area, or class expectations and desires.
Student learning profiles	The teacher collects self-reported information from students about their preferred learning activities and styles (such as visual, auditory, kinesthetic, analytical, or practical), the circumstances and conditions under which they learn best, and ways in which they prefer to express themselves (for example, writing, oral communication, physical expression, artistic media, and others).
Life connections	The teacher plans breaks during instructional time so that students can identify and discuss links between the content they are studying and their own personal experiences, hobbies, and interests. Students look for and explain similarities and differences between their interests and experiences and the content using metaphors and analogies.
Informal linkages during class discussion	The teacher becomes familiar with students' interests and personal experiences. As the class discusses topics, the teacher relates the content to existing knowledge about students' lives.

Source: Adapted from Marzano Resources, 2016cc.

The strategies in table 7.9 provide a broad array of options for the teacher. The teacher can use the strategy informal linkages during class discussion on a continuing basis as opportunities arise. For example, while addressing content about the topic of polynomials, the teacher might note that one of the students in class keeps track of ratings for college quarterbacks. The teacher asks the student to research and report on the equations that are used to compute the ratings, reminding the student that these equations are polynomials. The strategy of life connections is similar in that time is set aside for students to identify links between the content being addressed in class and anything in which they are interested. For example, while studying the structure of a healthy cell, one student might liken it to the *Starship Enterprise* while another might liken it to a winning football team. Students have to explain and justify the connections they have made. Other strategies require more preparation on the teacher's part. For example, student learning profiles require the teacher to take time to identify students' learning preferences and then use that information to make instruction more personally relevant to students.

When the strategies in this element produce the desired effects, teachers will observe the following behaviors in students.

- Students engage in activities that help them make connections between their personal interests and the content.
- Students can explain how making connections between content and their personal interests makes class more interesting and enhances their content knowledge.
- Students describe class as being relevant to them personally.

Element 32: Motivating and Inspiring Students

As its title indicates, this element directly focuses on high levels of motivation with the ultimate goal of inspiration. Motivation and inspiration occur when students have opportunities to be self-actualized and when they have opportunities to be connected to something greater than self. *Self-actualization* means that students feel like they are becoming more of whom they want to be in the future. *Connection to something greater than self* means that students feel like they are a part of something important. The strategies for this element appear in table 7.10.

Table 7.10: Motivating and Inspiring Students

Strategy	Description
Academic goal setting	The teacher helps students identify academic goals they want to accomplish over the course of a unit, semester, or year. The teacher then works with students to help them identify specific actions and smaller, short-term goals that, if completed, will help them accomplish their long-term goals.
Growth mindset cultivation	The teacher explicitly addresses the concept of the growth mindset, championed by Carol Dweck (2006). People with growth mindsets believe that they can increase their intelligence or abilities through hard work. On the other hand, those with a fixed mindset feel that intelligence is innate and cannot be changed, regardless of effort. The teacher explains this concept to students and provides opportunities for students to analyze the extent to which they are cultivating it in themselves.
Possible selves activities	The teacher provides students with opportunities to imagine what they could develop into later in life. Without such considerations, students may not be cognizant of the full range of possibilities available to them nor recognize that they can achieve certain possible selves that previously seemed off limits or unattainable.
Personal projects	The teacher uses personal projects to encourage students' desire for personal growth. In order for personal projects to be successful, however, students must select topics they are truly interested in and excited about. Personal projects often relate to broader life or long-term goals rather than academic content.
Altruism projects	Altruism projects encourage students to connect to something greater than themselves. The teacher has students brainstorm aspects of their community that they are interested in getting involved with. Once they have a list, the teacher can either group students interested in similar things together or have the whole class decide on one project from the list to address as a whole class. The teacher provides help but takes care not to lead the project, as this takes ownership away from the students.

continued →

Strategy	Description
Gratitude journals	The teacher uses gratitude journals to help students recognize the positive things in their lives. When introducing gratitude journals, the teacher first models the behavior by listing a few things that he or she is grateful for and recording them somewhere visible in the room or in his or her own personal gratitude journal. Students then brainstorm a few things they are grateful for individually, in small groups, or as a class and record their items in their own gratitude journals.
Mindfulness practice	Mindfulness is the practice of being aware of thoughts, feelings, and one's internal and external world. To exemplify mindfulness, the teacher asks students at the beginning of each class period to write down their intention for the class at the top of their notes. The teacher occasionally asks students to recall their intention. The teacher may also engage students in deep breathing, quick guided meditation, or other practices to help them refocus their thoughts.
Inspirational media	Inspiration occurs when a person sees evidence that one of his or her ideals—a belief that represents how an individual would like the world to be—is true. The teacher exposes students to an inspirational story and then has students discuss what ideal the story exemplifies.

Source: Adapted from Marzano Resources, 2016u.

Some of the strategies in table 7.10 deal directly with self-actualization. The most concrete of these is personal projects. During these projects, students set long-term goals they want to accomplish. For example, one student might set the long-term goal of making the track team in the spring. Another student might set the long-term goal of getting into an Ivy League college. The teacher sets aside time during the school week for all students to work on their projects.

Some of the strategies deal more directly with connection to something greater than self. For example, consider altruism projects. As their name implies, these projects provide opportunities for students to engage in activities that help others less fortunate. During a particular semester, a teacher might ask students to find a project that helps others in some way. One student might volunteer in her church. Another might find ways to help a family in the neighborhood that is experiencing financial difficulty. Periodically, students report about their projects and what they have learned from their involvement.

When the strategies in this element produce the desired effects, teachers will observe the following behaviors in students.

- Students set long-term goals and identify steps they must take to accomplish them.
- Students engage with community members in meaningful ways.
- Students work on projects of their own design that are meaningful to them.
- Students describe the class as *motivating* or *inspiring*.

Planning

The design question pertaining to using engagement strategies is, What engagement strategies will I use to help students pay attention, be energized, be intrigued, and be inspired? The ten elements that pertain to this design area provide specific guidance regarding this overall design question. Teachers can easily turn these elements into more focused planning questions.

- **Element 23:** What will I do to notice and react when students are not engaged?
- **Element 24:** What will I do to increase students' response rates?
- **Element 25:** What will I do to increase students' physical movement?
- **Element 26:** What will I do to maintain a lively pace?
- **Element 27:** What will I do to demonstrate intensity and enthusiasm?
- **Element 28:** What will I do to present unusual information?

- **Element 29:** What will I do to engage students in friendly controversy?
- **Element 30:** What will I do to engage students in academic games?
- **Element 31:** What will I do to provide opportunities for students to talk about themselves?
- **Element 32:** What will I do to motivate and inspire students?

Planning for engagement requires a great many decisions since a teacher would certainly not use all ten elements of this design area in a single unit of instruction. There are some, however, that the teacher would probably use frequently, if not every day, including:

- Noticing and reacting when students not engaged
- Increasing response rates
- Using physical movement
- Maintaining a lively pace
- Demonstrating intensity and enthusiasm

Teachers might use the others in more of a staggered fashion. For example, a teacher might plan to start students' long-term projects in the beginning of the school year and provide time for students to work on them throughout the year. A teacher might use the strategy of future possible selves in a more short-term manner. During the first quarter, the teacher provides information and activities that help support the concept of future possible selves. This would form a strong motivational foundation for future activities. Near the end of the year, the teacher might ask students to engage in altruistic projects. The teacher embeds other strategies in various units of instruction as needed. When planning for a unit, the teacher considers strategies from elements like friendly controversy, academic games, and presenting unusual information, selecting those that seem to best fit the content.

Implications for Change

The major implication for change regarding this design area is to make finer distinctions in terms of the various levels and types of engagement. Attention might be thought of as the most basic level of engagement. This simply means that students are aware of the activities occurring in class and choosing to participate in those activities. This type of engagement has long been an explicit goal for K–12 educators. A level up from attention is being energized. One way to think about this level is that classroom activities actually produce energy in students. While this too has been a goal of K–12 education, in my experience, classroom observations indicate that there is great variability in the extent to which teachers achieve or even aspire to this level. All too often, classrooms appear to decrease students' energy levels as opposed to enhancing them. Intrigue might be considered a level of engagement higher than being energized. At the very least, it is a different form of engagement. Intrigue is certainly an ideal to which educators subscribe. Again, in my experience, teachers rarely achieve this ideal most probably because of the strong emphasis on covering a large number of standards (discussed in chapter 1) as opposed to stimulating a sense of wonder in perhaps a small number of topics that would lead to an intrinsic desire to explore a broader array of topics. Motivation and inspiration surely represent the highest level of engagement because they deal with activities that make students feel actualized and connected to something greater than themselves (see Marzano, Scott, Boogren, & Newcomb, 2017). This is perhaps the operational definition of *intrinsic motivation*.

This enhanced view of engagement would surely stimulate many initiatives in schools and classrooms. Educators are currently satisfied if students are simply paying attention; they should surely be challenged to, on a regular basis, make their classrooms places that students leave more motivated than when they entered.

CHAPTER 8

Implementing Rules and Procedures

Part of a mental set conducive to learning is the perception that the classroom environment is orderly and safe. The teacher fosters such a perception through well-articulated rules and procedures.

> The desired mental states and processes for this design area are:
>
> Students understand and follow rules and procedures.

The following elements are important to effective rules and procedures.

Element 33: Establishing Rules and Procedures

The initiating element for this design area is establishing rules and procedures. This, of course, typically occurs at the beginning of the year, although teachers should make adaptations regarding rules and procedures throughout the year. The strategies for this element appear in table 8.1.

Table 8.1: Establishing Rules and Procedures

Strategy	Description
Using a small set of rules and procedures	Classroom rules and procedures are fundamental to building a productive learning community. The teacher prioritizes rules and procedures by restricting them to five to eight per class. Generally, a teacher should begin the year by establishing general classroom rules, then work toward procedures for more specific areas such as the beginning and end of the school day or period, transitions, and the efficient use of materials and equipment.
Explaining rules and procedures to students	At the beginning of the school year or term, the teacher takes time to explain each of the rules and why he or she chose them. The teacher and students make rules more explicit by creating procedures (how-to steps) for them. These how-to steps are often referred to as standard operating procedures, or SOPs.

continued →

Strategy	Description
Generating rules and procedures with students	The teacher devotes class time to designing rules and procedures from the ground up. The teacher shifts responsibility to the entire class for crafting the classroom SOPs.
Modifying rules and procedures with students	The teacher presents general rules to the class and asks students to operationalize them by coming up with specific behaviors or procedures for each rule. The teacher lists the student-generated procedures underneath each general rule and prominently posts them in the classroom for future reference.
Reviewing rules and procedures with students	Periodically, the teacher has students review rules and procedures. If students seem to systematically violate or ignore rules and procedures, the teacher calls the lapse to students' attention and reviews and models the rule or procedure as necessary.
Using the language of responsibility and statements of school beliefs	The teacher leads a discussion about concepts like freedom, equality, responsibility, threats, opinions, and rights. After introducing, defining, and discussing these and other relevant terms, the teacher uses the terms consistently to describe and discuss classroom behavior.
Posting rules around the room	The teacher posts rules around the classroom as both a visual reminder for students and as a way to hold students accountable for their behavior. The teacher posts the general classroom rules in a prominent location where students can frequently and easily see them; rules and procedures for specific areas or activities should be posted near their relevant locations.
Writing a class pledge or classroom constitution	The teacher initiates a classroom pledge. It is an informal contract—when students sign it, they are promising to follow the rules that the teacher and the class have set. Students should be directly involved in writing the class pledge or constitution based on the classroom rules and procedures.
Using posters and graphics	The teacher uses posters and graphics to display rules, procedures, and character traits. This helps students better remember them while simultaneously decorating the classroom. These posters and graphics emphasize the importance of specific rules and procedures or specific character traits important to proper classroom functioning (integrity, emotional control, and so on).
Establishing gestures and symbols	Within the classroom, teachers and students need to communicate some messages frequently, such as "quiet down" or "I need help with this assignment." The teacher and students collaborate to establish gestures or symbols that communicate these common messages quickly and efficiently.
Modeling with vignettes and role playing	The teacher has students model rules and procedures through role playing. A teacher might divide the class into small groups and assign two groups to each classroom rule or procedure. One group would create a skit that demonstrates a nonexample of a rule or procedure. The other group would act out correct adherence to the rule.
Holding classroom meetings	Classroom meetings are a time for students and the teacher to discuss how the classroom is functioning and identify how it might run more smoothly. The teacher and students bring up issues relative to classroom management, including rules and procedures. Students might raise issues for discussion verbally during this time, or the teacher might ask students to suggest issues beforehand or submit them in a suggestion box for discussion during classroom meetings.
Implementing student self-assessment	The teacher periodically asks students to assess their own level of adherence to classroom rules and procedures. To do so, the teacher simply presents students with rules or procedures and asks them to rate their adherence to those rules and procedures on a scale of 0 (not adhering) to 4 (exemplary adherence).

Source: Adapted from Marzano Resources, 2016l.

A few strategies in table 8.1 deal with the teacher overseeing the construction of rules and procedures. For example, consider the strategy of using a small set of rules and procedures. This is a management function in which the teacher ensures that the number of rules and procedures does not become so large as to hinder execution. Typically about five to eight are recommended.

Some strategies deal with students understanding how to use rules and procedures and why they are important. To illustrate, consider the strategy of explaining rules and procedures to students. This is an appropriate foundational activity since student compliance is not the goal of rules and procedures. Rather, the goal is for students to perceive the classroom environment as safe and orderly. For this to happen, students must understand the reasons why they must follow certain rules and procedures.

Many strategies are intended to maximize students' sense of ownership of rules and procedures. For example, consider the strategy of writing a class pledge or classroom constitution. Here the class as a whole designs a set of statements about behavior to which it is willing to commit. Such actions move students to a volitional level as opposed to a compliance level when it comes to rules and procedures.

When the strategies in this element produce the desired effects, teachers will observe the following behaviors in students.

- Students can describe established rules and procedures.
- Students describe the classroom as an orderly place.
- Students regulate their own behavior.

Element 34: Organizing the Physical Layout of the Classroom

Some teachers overlook the classroom's physical layout while others pay a great deal of attention to this element. The latter position is the more desirable of the two because the classroom's physical layout and appearance can enhance or hinder students' perceptions of order. Strategies associated with the physical layout address decorations, materials, and areas for instruction as well as the ease with which teachers can monitor what is occurring. Specific strategies for this element appear in table 8.2.

Table 8.2: Organizing the Physical Layout of the Classroom

Strategy	Description
Designing classroom décor	The teacher posts pictures, posters, and homelike touches (such as curtains) or uses themes relevant to the season or upcoming events to make the classroom feel friendly. The teacher aligns the classroom décor with learning goals and instructional priorities, so that it enforces the value and relevance of what students are learning.
Displaying student work	It is important for students to see themselves represented in the classroom. As such, the teacher considers how to display students' work within the classroom and how such displays reinforce learning. A teacher can either post the same assignment from all class members or post particularly noteworthy assignments from individual students.
Considering classroom materials	The teacher monitors learning materials and ensures that students can easily access and organize them. The teacher considers the placement and organization of various classroom materials as well as the frequency of their use. Frequently used materials should be in a location that allows for easy access and should be organized and labeled in such a way that students can find what they need quickly and independently. Teachers can store less frequently used materials in a less accessible space, bringing them out for students when necessary.
Placing the teacher's desk	The teacher considers desk placement and use during class time. Ideally, a teacher's desk placement allows him or her to monitor the class during seatwork and is easily accessible during whole-group instruction.

continued →

Strategy	Description
Placing student desks	The teacher considers how students may use desks during whole-class, small-group, and individual instruction. The arrangement of students' desks should allow students to hear directions, watch instruction, access necessary materials, and move quickly and safely around the classroom.
Planning areas for whole-group instruction	The teacher considers the ease of access to materials students frequently use during whole-group instruction, the teacher's ability to instruct and monitor the class, and students' ability to hear the teacher and see the board.
Planning areas for group work	The teacher considers where small groups of students can meet and how easy this is considering student desk placement. The teacher also creates a space where he or she can meet with a small group of students while the rest of the class completes individual seatwork.
Planning learning centers	The teacher considers the location of learning centers. A learning center should be easy to monitor from all parts of the room and should be close to books, resources, and other materials that may be required to complete tasks at the center.
Considering computers and technology equipment	Many classrooms have their own computer or computer stations to which students have access. When designing the physical layout of a classroom, the teacher considers the various technologies in his or her classroom, their purposes, and how students make use of them.
Considering lab equipment and supplies	Most science teachers will have to consider effective storage and use of lab equipment and supplies. When making these decisions, the teacher considers student safety, protection for the equipment, and ease of access and use for students.
Planning classroom libraries	The teacher locates libraries that will provide support for individual, small-group, and whole-group learning activities. The primary concern with regard to bookshelves is that their location provides easy access but does not cause traffic jams.
Involving students in the design process	The teacher asks students to be involved in designing the classroom. The teacher may informally poll students to solicit their feedback about the classroom décor and organization or formally survey them.

Source: Adapted from Marzano Resources, 2016x.

Some of the strategies in table 8.2 involve things that the teacher can and should do to make the physical environment as positive as possible for students. For example, the strategy designing classroom décor involves the teacher trying to make the classroom physically appealing to students through the use of color, pictures, and decorations of various sorts.

Many strategies address classroom logistics. For example, desk placement can enhance student learning, just as proper space for whole-class and small-group instruction can.

Some of the strategies offer students a voice and choice in how to organize the classroom. For example, involving students in the design process ensures that they have some decision-making power about the physical layout of the classroom.

When the strategies in this element produce the desired effects, teachers will observe the following behaviors in students.

- Students move easily about the classroom.
- Students make use of materials and learning centers.
- Students access and use examples of their work the teacher has displayed.
- Students access and use the information on bulletin boards.
- Students can easily focus on instruction.

Element 35: Demonstrating Withitness

The field of education has widely used the term *withitness* since Jacob Kounin (1970, 1983) coined it. Basically, *withitness* means that a teacher is alert and aware of what is occurring in the classroom at all times. This helps teachers identify possible disruptive behaviors and proactively address them. The specific strategies for this element appear in table 8.3.

Table 8.3: Demonstrating Withitness

Strategy	Description
Being proactive	The teacher takes steps to become aware of what could potentially go wrong or cause disruption in class and pre-emptively takes actions to avoid such scenarios from occurring. For example, the teacher might confer privately with potentially disruptive students to review classroom expectations, create contingency plans for various behavior scenarios that might be likely to arise throughout the day, or seek out information regarding incidents that have occurred outside of class that may affect student behavior.
Occupying the whole room physically and visually	The teacher makes eye contact regularly with each student to let the student know he or she is aware of the student's actions and is monitoring the classroom. Furthermore, the teacher spends time in each quadrant of the room on a regular basis and physically moves through the classroom during instruction and individual seatwork.
Noticing potential problems	The teacher takes action to identify and pre-emptively address situations that could develop into larger disruptive behaviors. The teacher might watch for small groups of students huddled together talking intensely or one or more students not engaging in a class activity for an extended period of time. The teacher takes appropriate actions to diffuse the potentially disruptive behavior before it escalates.
Using a series of graduated actions	When noticing disruptive behavior, the teacher makes eye contact with those students involved in the incident or who exhibit the behavior. If the problem persists, the teacher stands right next to the offending student or students and uses nonverbal cues to communicate that they need to stop their inappropriate behavior and join in what the class is doing. If the behavior still persists, the teacher talks to the offending students quietly and privately. If the behavior does not stop, the teacher stops the class and calmly and politely addresses the disruption.

Source: Adapted from Marzano Resources, 2016h.

Withitness is sometimes incorrectly thought of as an innate ability that one either has or does not have; in fact, it is more behavioral than dispositional. That is, one can become "with it" by engaging in specific behaviors such as those listed in table 8.3. To a great extent, withitness is a matter of creating the perception in students that the teacher is aware of everything that is happening in class. Simple behaviors like occupying all parts of a classroom or looking students in the eye can produce these perceptions.

Some strategies in table 8.3 operate more on the teacher's level of awareness than on actual classroom behavior. For example, consider the strategy of being proactive. Here, the teacher systematically thinks about the students in his or her classes, trying to discern any potential needs they might have that, if left unmet, could cause the students to act out in class. The ultimate behavioral strategy involves using a series of graduated actions in which the teacher begins by making sure potentially disruptive students have come under the teacher's scrutiny. If the potentially disruptive behavior does not cease, the teacher increases the obtrusiveness of his or her corrective actions until finally ceasing instruction and addressing the issue publicly.

When the strategies in this element produce the desired effects, teachers will observe the following behaviors in students.

- Students recognize that the teacher is aware of their behavior.
- Students describe the teacher as aware of what is going on.
- Students extinguish potentially disruptive behaviors quickly and efficiently.

Element 36: Acknowledging Adherence to Rules and Procedures

Following or not following rules and procedures are decisions students make. When they make a decision to follow them, the teacher should acknowledge it. Acknowledgement from the teacher not only provides students with positive reinforcement for their decisions but also communicates gratitude. Specific strategies for this element appear in table 8.4.

Table 8.4: Acknowledging Adherence to Rules and Procedures

Strategy	Description
Verbal affirmation	The teacher uses short verbal affirmations such as "thank you," "good job," "that's great," or "very good" to acknowledge adherence to rules and procedures. The teacher might also have short conversations with students to acknowledge their adherence to rules and procedures.
Nonverbal affirmation	The teacher uses a smile, a wink, a nod of the head, a thumbs-up, an OK sign (thumb and forefinger loop), a pantomimed tip of the hat, a pat on the back, or a high-five to acknowledge students' adherence to rules and procedures.
Tangible recognition	The teacher uses privileges, activities, or items as positive consequences for following rules and procedures.
Token economies	The teacher uses a system in which students receive a token, chit (voucher), or points when they meet expectations. They can then exchange these tokens, chits, or points for privileges, activities, or items.
Daily recognition form	The teacher awards each student a starting score at the beginning of class (for example, twenty points) for a prearranged set of expectations (for example, four points for punctuality, four points for preparation, four points for on-task behavior, four points for respectfulness, and four points for work completion). If a student fails to meet a particular expectation, the teacher takes away some or all of the points associated with that expectation.
Color-coded behavior	The teacher gives each student three cards (red card = unacceptable behavior, yellow card = acceptable behavior with room for improvement, green card = exceptional adherence to rules and procedures) to keep on his or her desktop. All students begin the day or period with the green card on top. If a student's behavior warrants it, the teacher changes the exposed card to indicate the behavior a student is exhibiting.
Certificates	The teacher uses reward certificates to increase parental involvement and awareness of behavior at school. A student who helps another student with work, for example, would receive a certificate as a special recognition of his or her helpfulness.
Phone calls, emails, and notes	The teacher makes phone calls and sends emails or notes to a student's parents or guardians to recognize positive behavior.

Source: Adapted from Marzano Resources, 2016a.

Some of the strategies in table 8.4 are short and simple forms of recognition. For example, verbal and nonverbal affirmations can be as straightforward as a teacher saying "thank you" or providing an affirmation for a rule or procedure followed well.

Some strategies are much more concrete, such as daily recognition forms or behavior certificates. Some teachers misunderstand token economy strategies to focus on rewards because students accrue points for adherence to rules and procedures. However, they more so focus on the development of positive behavioral habits. The points are symbols of behavioral growth as opposed to rewards.

When the strategies in this element produce the desired effects, teachers will observe the following behaviors in students.

- Students appear appreciative of the teacher's acknowledgement.
- Students describe the teacher as aware of their good behavior.
- Students regularly adhere to rules and procedures.

Element 37: Acknowledging Lack of Adherence to Rules and Procedures

Just as the teacher should acknowledge students' decisions to adhere to rules and procedures, so should he or she acknowledge in some way students' decisions not to adhere to rules and procedures. However, such acknowledgement should not come in the form of punishment. The strategies for this element appear in table 8.5.

Table 8.5: Acknowledging Lack of Adherence to Rules and Procedures

Strategy	Description
Verbal cues	The teacher says a student's name, quietly reminds a student that he or she is not following a rule or procedure, quietly states the expected appropriate behavior, or simply tells a student to stop the current behavior.
Pregnant pause	The teacher stops teaching in response to recurring disruptive behavior, creating an uncomfortable silence that will direct the attention in the room toward the misbehaving student.
Nonverbal cues	The teacher uses eye contact, proximity, subtle gestures (such as shaking the head "no," putting a finger on the lips, tapping a student's desk, giving a thumbs-down, or raising eyebrows) to signal to a student that his or her behavior is inappropriate.
Time-out	The teacher asks an offending student to go to a designated place (inside or outside the classroom) until the student is ready to resume regular classroom activities. The teacher might use a graduated three-step process for sending a student to time out: (1) warning; (2) time-out inside the classroom, where the student can continue to attend to the academic activities that are occurring; and (3) time-out outside the classroom.
Overcorrection	The teacher requires a student who has behaved destructively to make things better than they were before the student destroyed them. If a student ruins class property, for example, the student would repair what was destroyed and then improve additional class property.
Interdependent group contingency	The teacher gives the entire class positive consequences only if every student in the class meets a certain behavioral standard. The teacher can use this type of group contingency to reinforce positive group behaviors and extinguish negative group behaviors.
Home contingency	To help an individual student perceive that his or her teacher and parents or guardians are unified in their attempt to help the student control his or her classroom behavior, the teacher meets with the student and parents or guardians to identify and discuss the student's use of inappropriate behavior in class.
High-intensity situation plan	The teacher articulates a plan for high-intensity situations. The plan includes assessing the severity of the situation, remaining calm, actively listening to the student's concerns, and removing the student from the situation once he or she has regained some control.
Overall disciplinary plan	The teacher creates an overall plan for dealing with disciplinary situations. It might include developing relationships with students, exhibiting withitness, articulating positive and negative consequences for behavior, and creating guidelines for dealing with high-intensity situations.

Source: Adapted from Marzano Resources, 2016b.

Some of the strategies in table 8.5 are basically reminders to students. For example, verbal and nonverbal cues let students know when they are about to misbehave. Some of the strategies involve consequences for inappropriate behaviors. For example, the time-out strategies involve temporarily separating from other students someone who is not following rules and procedures. Some of the strategies involve support and positive pressure from other students. For example, interdependent group contingency strategies organize students in groups who hold each other accountable for good behavior.

When the strategies in this element produce the desired effects, teachers will observe the following behaviors in students.

- Students cease inappropriate behavior following the teacher cues.
- Students accept consequences for their behavior as a natural part of the way the class is conducted.
- Students describe the teacher as *fair* relative to the consequences for not following rules and procedures.

Planning

The design question pertaining to implementing rules and procedures is, What strategies will I use to help students understand and follow rules and procedures? The five elements that pertain to this design area provide specific guidance regarding this overall design question. Teachers can easily turn these elements into more focused planning questions.

- **Element 33:** What will I do to establish rules and procedures?
- **Element 34:** What will I do to make the physical layout of the classroom most conducive to learning?
- **Element 35:** What will I do to demonstrate withitness?
- **Element 36:** What will I do to acknowledge adherence to rules and procedures?
- **Element 37:** What will I do to acknowledge lack of adherence to rules and procedures?

Planning for effective use of rules and procedures begins with elements 33 and 34. This makes intuitive sense. Teachers should establish rules and procedures with student input at the very beginning of the year. At the same time, the teacher must address the physical layout of the classroom. Teachers should continually update both rules and procedures and the physical layout of the classroom. Demonstrating withitness, acknowledging adherence to rules and procedures, and acknowledging lack of adherence to rules and procedures are not planned for so much as they are prepared for. That is, a teacher should utilize strategies in these areas as needed to continually monitor and refine rules and procedures.

Implications for Change

Rules and procedures are a staple of K–12 education. It might seem that little change could or should occur in this arena. In fact, this area is ripe for a major shift from being teacher directed to being student directed. Instead of the teacher imposing rules that the class must follow, students should become the architects of rules and procedures. This is most obvious in the steps referred to as *SOPs*, or *standard operating procedures*. They are the vehicle to explain rules and procedures to students and generate rules and procedures with students (see figure 8.1, page 87). To illustrate, figure 8.1 contains an SOP for determining what a student may have missed from being absent.

How can I determine what I missed?

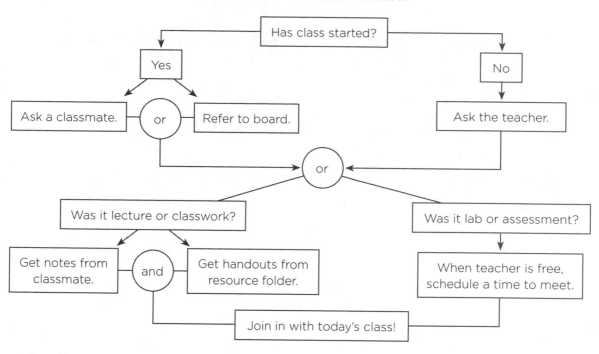

Source: Adapted from Marzano et al., 2017.

Figure 8.1: SOP for determining what a student has missed.

Students should generate SOPs, like the one in figure 8.1. If students design and implement SOPs, the classroom eventually evolves to a culture in which students are as responsible and accountable as the teacher for establishing a positive learning environment. I believe such a process is one of the most important things teachers can do to develop student agency.

CHAPTER 9

Building Relationships

Important aspects of a mental context conducive to learning are a sense of being welcome and that teachers and peers value basic human needs. When these needs are satisfied, a student feels relaxed and comfortable. Teachers can create this perception in students by focusing on teacher-to-student relationships and student-to-student relationships.

> The desired mental states and processes regarding relationships are:
> Students feel welcome, accepted, and valued.

The following elements are important to building effective relationships.

Element 38: Using Verbal and Nonverbal Behaviors That Indicate Affection for Students

One of the most straightforward ways to provide students with a sense that they are welcome, accepted, and valued is to engage in behaviors that demonstrate such sentiments. There are a number of strategies teachers can use to accomplish this. The specific strategies for this element appear in table 9.1.

Table 9.1: Using Verbal and Nonverbal Behaviors That Indicate Affection for Students

Strategy	Description
Greeting students at the classroom door	At the beginning of a period, the teacher greets students at the door. The teacher uses students' first names when they enter to show that the teacher values them and is aware of when they are present. The teacher might also ask students how they are feeling and make positive comments about their learning or achievements.
Holding informal conferences	Informal conferences, unlike more formal academic conferences, allow teachers and students to chat without students projecting expectations onto the meeting. During informal conferences, a teacher might give compliments, ask for student opinions, mention student successes, and pass on positive comments from other teachers.

continued →

Strategy	Description
Attending after-school functions	The teacher shows affection for and interest in students, particularly students who may feel alienated, by attending their after-school activities. If attending, the teacher lets the student know ahead of time and then makes an effort to connect with the student at the event, if possible.
Greeting students by name outside of school	The teacher takes advantage of encounters with students or their parents outside of school hours in neighborhood venues such as the grocery store, movie theater, or shopping mall. When this occurs, the teacher greets students by name and interacts with a friendly demeanor.
Giving students special responsibilities or leadership roles in the classroom	The teacher assigns students to specific tasks or responsibilities in the classroom. Specific tasks or responsibilities for students might include being a line leader on the way to lunch, taking care of a class pet, handing out materials, or collecting assignments. If a student's previous actions have warranted it, the teacher might give the student a leadership role in the classroom, which can further demonstrate that the teacher both cares for and trusts the student.
Scheduling interaction	The teacher creates a schedule that ensures regular interaction with each student by selecting a few students each day to seek out and talk to. The teacher might interact with students in the lunchroom, during breaks between classes, or right after school.
Creating a photo bulletin board	The teacher creates a bulletin board that displays students' photos, personal goals, hobbies, interests, and other fun facts. The content of photo bulletin boards can change based on the unit or can highlight students who have performed well on assignments, shown dramatic improvement on a learning goal, or enacted classroom values outside of class.
Using physical behaviors	The teacher monitors his or her physical behaviors and gestures to ensure that they signal affection and encouragement for students. The teacher might use smiles and high-fives, for example, to communicate affection for students, while patting a student on the back or putting a hand on a student's shoulder to communicate interest or concern.
Using humor	The teacher uses humor strategically. The teacher can use playful banter, jokes, or self-directed humor. The teacher might also use historical and popular sayings to make a point or incorporate cartoons, jokes, puns, and wordplay into instruction.

Source: Adapted from Marzano Resources, 2016qq.

Some of the strategies in table 9.1 focus on developing positive relationships between teachers and students. For example, greeting students at the door and by name are easy but effective ways of signaling to students that the teacher cares for them.

Some strategies provide students with the sense that their peers value them. For example, photo bulletin boards display information about each student in class, allowing them to see each other's accomplishments and interests.

When the strategies in this element produce the desired effects, teachers will observe the following behaviors in students.

- Students describe the teacher as someone who cares for them.
- Students describe the classroom as a friendly place.
- Students respond to the teacher's verbal interactions.
- Students respond to the teacher's nonverbal interactions.

Element 39: Understanding Students' Backgrounds and Interests

The strategies within this element help build students' perception that their teacher and peers respect them. This is accomplished by structuring activities that subtly disclose each student's accomplishments, likes, and dislikes. The specific strategies for this element appear in table 9.2.

Table 9.2: Understanding Students' Backgrounds and Interests

Strategy	Description
Student background surveys	At the start of the school year or beginning of a course, the teacher gives a background questionnaire containing questions relevant to students' lives. The survey includes questions about students' academic interests (favorite and least favorite subject in school), personal interests (hobbies, sports, lessons, art, books, video games, movies, and television shows), dreams, fears, family members, and family activities (traditions, vacations, and gatherings).
Opinion questionnaires	The teacher uses opinion questionnaires, like student background surveys, to better understand students' perspectives and backgrounds. However, opinion questionnaires generally focus on relevant classroom topics. For example, a teacher might create an opinion questionnaire that asks students the degree to which the classroom content is interesting and relevant. The questionnaire might also subtly gauge students' feelings of competence related to specific tasks.
Individual teacher-student conferences	The teacher schedules individual teacher-student conferences. In an individual teacher-student conference, the teacher covers both academic and nonacademic subjects to better understand the student.
Parent-teacher conferences	The teacher schedules parent-teacher conferences. During such conferences, the teacher identifies events of note, which might include family events or vacations and transition points for parents or siblings (such as births, deaths, graduations, marriages, divorces, or job changes).
School newspaper, newsletter, or bulletin	Many schools have publications, either for students or for parents, that showcase students' notable achievements. The teacher reads these publications to become aware of students' involvement in athletic events (such as track or swim meets; basketball, baseball, football, or other sports; and awards ceremonies), debates, club events, school performances, and volunteer activities.
Informal class interviews	Informal class interviews occur when a teacher asks students to share information about what is happening at school or in their lives about which the teacher should be aware. The teacher asks specific questions that prompt students to talk about their lives. Before starting direct instruction on a Monday, for example, the teacher might ask the students to share what they did over the weekend.
Familiarity with student culture	The teacher talks with students and becomes familiar with popular cultural phenomena students are interested in. This may include popular music, movies, television shows, specific actors, singers, or bands.
Autobiographical metaphors and analogies	The teacher has students construct metaphors that compare academic content with their own lives. This strategy provides a teacher with knowledge about students' backgrounds while simultaneously strengthening students' understanding of the content.
Six-word autobiographies	The teacher has students write an autobiography in exactly six words, and the teacher leads a discussion in which students share and explain their autobiographies. The six-word autobiographies can be either a disparate list of six words (particularly for younger students) or a functioning sentence.
Independent investigations	The teacher has students research a topic of interest to them and then report back to the class about their findings. These investigations can relate to class content or be driven by students' nonacademic interests.
Quotes	The teacher asks students to collect quotes that they feel express their personality traits, interests, or aspirations. Then students share the quotes they find, which helps the teacher better understand students' personalities and interests.

continued →

Strategy	Description
Comments about student achievement or areas of importance	Once a teacher has some background knowledge about students' values and interests, he or she notices and comments on individual accomplishments and important events in their lives. In terms of individual accomplishments, a teacher might point out students' achievements in clubs or athletics, academic recognitions, artistic and dramatic accomplishments, or assignments done well.
Lineups	The teacher uses specific questions that ask students to line up or sit in groups in ways that reveal their likes, dislikes, and preferences. Questions can be playful and serve as a fun activity to get to know students' personalities, be academically oriented to help the teacher better understand students' learning preferences, or both.
Individual student learning goals	The teacher asks students to identify something that interests them during instruction and create their own personalized learning goals during a unit. The teacher helps students connect their personalized learning goals to teacher-identified learning goals.

Source: Adapted from Marzano Resources, 2016mm.

Some strategies in table 9.2 help the teacher acquire information about students' backgrounds and interests. For example, consider the strategies of student background surveys and parent-teacher conferences. Surveys are a very overt way to learn about students. Parent-teacher conferences are a little more subtle in that a teacher tries to glean information from the conversation that would promote conversations that make students feel welcome.

Some strategies help students discover more about each other. For example, consider the strategy of school newspapers, newsletters, and bulletins. They all represent ways to share student accomplishments with classmates. Weekly or monthly, these strategies single out and feature students.

When the strategies in this element produce the desired effects, teachers will observe the following behaviors in students.

- Students describe the teacher as someone who knows them or is interested in them.
- Students respond when the teacher demonstrates understanding of their interests and backgrounds.
- Students say they feel that their teacher values them.
- Students say they know their peers.

Element 40: Displaying Objectivity and Control

This element focuses on teacher behaviors that help students perceive the teacher as someone who will not be angry with them if they misbehave, but who will enforce rules and procedures in an objective and unemotional manner. The strategies for this element appear in table 9.3.

Table 9.3: Displaying Objectivity and Control

Strategy	Description
Self-reflection	The teacher self-reflects daily about consistency when enforcing the positive and negative consequences associated with the established rules and procedures. Questions the teacher might consider include the following: Did I provide proper acknowledgement when students followed the rules and procedures? Did I use proper consequences when students did not follow rules and procedures? Did I take every opportunity today to provide positive and negative consequences for student behavior?
Self-monitoring	The teacher monitors his or her emotions in the classroom to avoid displaying counterproductive emotions such as anger, frustration, or hesitation. Before class each day, the teacher mentally reviews all of his or her students, noting those who might cause problems.

Strategy	Description
Emotional triggers	The teacher considers sources of stress and other emotional triggers that make it hard for him or her to maintain emotional objectivity. Such triggers might be personal events, certain times of the school year, or specific student or faculty behaviors that make the teacher feel a certain way.
Self-care	Self-care is the intentional actions or practices that an individual partakes in to ensure his or her physical, mental, or emotional health. To engage in self-care, the teacher identifies activities that he or she finds rewarding and healthy and engages in the activities as needed to mitigate negative feelings.
Assertiveness	When interacting with students, a teacher may be assertive, passive, or aggressive. Ideally, a teacher should aim to be assertive—able to assert his or her own needs without ignoring or violating the rights of his or her students. As such, an assertive teacher navigates classroom relationships in a way that shows respect for students while still demonstrating that he or she has control.
A cool exterior	The teacher maintains a cool exterior when dealing with conflicts in the classroom. Maintaining a cool exterior includes using assertive body language, self-monitoring facial expressions, speaking in a calm and respectful tone of voice, actively listening to reasonable explanations, and avoiding engagement with students who argue, deny, or blame others for their conduct.
Active listening and speaking	The teacher listens to students without agreeing or disagreeing. The teacher focuses on what the student is saying and tries to understand the student's viewpoint. The teacher stays neutral in body posture, gesture, and facial expression.
Communication styles	The teacher monitors his or her communication styles. Generally, communication styles fall into the following five categories: (1) assertive connector, (2) apathetic avoider, (3) junior therapist, (4) bulldozer, and (5) hider. The teacher becomes aware of various communication styles, determines the communication style he or she uses the most, and assesses how this style affects the relationships in the classroom.
Unique student needs	Five types of students have unique needs that may challenge a teacher's ability to remain objective and in control: students who (1) are passive, (2) are aggressive, (3) have attention problems, (4) are perfectionistic, and (5) are socially inept. The teacher considers students in his or her classes and identifies who may have unique needs. Once the teacher identifies such students, he or she takes proactive steps in remaining objective and in control during interactions with these students.

Source: Adapted from Marzano Resources, 2016i.

Many strategies in table 9.3 focus on the teacher being aware of his or her own tendencies to lose control or interact with students in ways that are not positive. For example, consider the strategy of self-reflection. This requires the teacher to identify those students for whom they often react negatively when those students misbehave. This awareness can help teachers remain calm and thoughtful when they are about to overreact to a negative incident with specific students.

Some strategies focus on behaviors that help ensure students stay calm during tense situations. For example, consider the strategy of active listening. Here the teacher employs specific techniques when a student has lost or is about to lose control. Active-listening strategies communicate to students that the teacher considers the student's feelings important because the teacher is clearly paying attention to what the student is saying.

When the strategies in this element produce the desired effects, teachers will observe the following behaviors in students.

- Students feel settled by the teacher's calm demeanor.
- Students describe the teacher as someone who is in control of himself or herself and in control of the class.
- Students say that the teacher does not hold grudges or take things personally.

Planning

The design question pertaining to building relationships is, What strategies will I use to help students feel welcome, accepted, and valued? The three elements that pertain to this design area provide specific guidance regarding this overall design question. Teachers can easily turn these elements into more focused planning questions.

- **Element 38:** How will I use verbal and nonverbal behaviors to indicate affection for students?
- **Element 39:** How will I demonstrate that I understand students' backgrounds and interests?
- **Element 40:** How will I demonstrate objectivity and control?

Teachers should plan for these elements on a *systematic basis*. That is, a teacher should periodically identify those things he or she will do to verbally and nonverbally communicate affection for all students. For example, a teacher might regularly think about her students and identify those with whom she cannot recall having a recent positive interaction. This does not necessarily mean that the teacher has had negative interactions with the identified students, but simply that the teacher can't remember any recent positive interactions. The teacher then makes a mental note to say something positive to the identified students the following day.

Relative to understanding students' backgrounds and interests, the teacher might identify those students about whose background she knows little. The teacher selects a specific student and designs ways she will find out more about the student, like simply having an informal conversation with the student at lunch time.

Relative to communicating objectivity and control, the teacher might identify those students that tend to irritate her, which, in turn, commonly leads to the teacher overreacting when those students don't follow rules and procedures. The teacher then devises a specific strategy she will employ to keep herself calm during those moments of agitation. The strategy might begin with the teacher reminding herself that she is probably already beginning to overreact and must do something to alter the normal set of actions she takes in situations like this.

Implications for Change

The main implication for change relative to relationships is shifting the process of forming a positive relationship with students from one of personal preference on the teachers' part to one of choice and specific actions. This involves teachers examining their perceptions of students.

In general, human beings form perceptions about the characteristics of those with whom we interact. If we like or admire those characteristics we perceive in others, we tend to seek out and cultivate positive relationships with them. We treat them in positive ways and they commonly reciprocate by treating us in positive ways (Marzano & Marzano, 2015).

This works well for most teachers because they tend to have a natural affinity for students at the age and grade levels they teach. Elementary teachers enjoy the constant questions their first graders ask and their need for compliments and even hugs on some occasions. Middle school teachers enjoy students' seemingly irrational behavior and the constant giggling they exhibit. High school teachers enjoy students' sometimes awkward and sometimes sophisticated attempts to be treated as adults.

In effect, it is easy for most teachers to form positive relationships with most students simply because the teachers have a predisposition to interpret students' behaviors in positive ways. But there are occasions when a teacher has a student whose behaviors he or she does not interpret positively. In these cases, establishing a positive relationship with the student is a matter of deciding to act in positive ways with the student even though the teacher is not inclined to do so.

Taken to their logical conclusions, these dynamics imply that teachers must behave in ways that communicate affection to all students, even those for whom they have no natural affinity. I believe that if this were the standard operating procedure in every classroom, schools would be places where every student felt a sense of belonging and esteem. This might go a long way toward enhancing student achievement, particularly for those who currently feel disenfranchised.

CHAPTER 10

Communicating High Expectations

The final component of developing an effective context for learning is to communicate high expectations for all students. The need for this focus comes directly from the literature on expectations. In the mid-20th century, researchers determined that teachers' expectations about how well students were going to perform in their classes influenced how they treated them (see Rosenthal, 1956; Rosenthal & Jacobson, 1968). The greater teachers' expectations for students, the more teachers challenge and interact with them. The lower the expectations, the less teachers challenge and interact with students. Unfortunately, it is difficult to be completely aware of one's expectations. However, it is very straightforward to ensure teachers treat all students equally and equitably.

In effect, teachers must pay special attention to students for whom educators wittingly or unwittingly have developed low expectations. It is not so much that these students need dramatically different strategies to feel valued and respected, but sometimes teachers don't use typical instructional strategies as rigorously or completely with these students as they do with other students.

> The desired mental states and processes for high expectations are:
>
> Typically reluctant students feel valued and do not hesitate to interact with the teacher or their peers.

It is important to note that I prefer to use the terms *reluctant students* or *reluctant learners* as opposed to *low-expectancy students*, even though the latter is more consistent with the research literature (see Marzano, 2007). The following elements are important to communicating high expectations for reluctant learners.

Element 41: Demonstrating Value and Respect for Reluctant Learners

One of the first steps to communicating high expectations for all students is to help them feel valued and respected. The strategies for this element appear in table 10.1 (page 98).

Table 10.1: Demonstrating Value and Respect for Reluctant Learners

Strategy	Description
Identifying expectation levels for all students	The first step toward demonstrating equal value and respect for all students is to identify pre-existing differences in student expectations. To do this, the teacher identifies the expectation level for each student by imagining that each student has completed a comprehensive assessment that covers some of the more difficult content addressed in class. On a class list, the teacher writes the level at which he or she expects each student to perform on such an assessment: high, average, or low.
Identifying differential treatment of reluctant learners	The teacher tracks his or her behavior for several days to increase awareness of differences in affective tone and quality of interaction with specific students. Using an informal observation form, the teacher keeps track of his or her affective tone and interaction quality with specific students.
Using nonverbal and verbal indicators of respect	The teacher uses eye contact, smiling, proximity, hand and body gestures, physical contact, and playful dialogue to communicate value and respect for all students. If the teacher recognizes different treatment for reluctant learners, the teacher makes an effort to use both verbal and nonverbal indicators to show respect and value for reluctant learners.

Source: Adapted from Marzano Resources, 2016g.

The first two strategies in table 10.1 provide teachers with the necessary awareness to ensure that reluctant learners are treated in a way that communicates high expectations. The first strategy (identifying expectation levels for all students) helps teachers become aware of the biases that may have crept into their thinking about students. For example, relatively early in the year, a teacher might scan students' names with the intent of identifying those who she thinks will not do well in class. This should be done with self-impunity in that the teacher should not be self-critical for having formed such conclusions. Forming conclusions about people is a natural human tendency. The teacher might also try to determine why she has formed these conclusions. This is where a teacher can detect bias. If the teacher notices that the students for whom she has low expectations all dress a certain way or talk a certain way, these would be biases. Again, this should be done with self-impunity. However, biases, although natural tendencies, are quite harmful; teachers should eradicate them as much as possible.

The second strategy (identifying differential treatment of reluctant learners) helps teachers become aware of the extent to which they treat reluctant students differently. This strategy requires some thought and effort because it involves a teacher comparing his or her treatment of reluctant students with treatment of high-expectancy students. All too often, teachers find that there are some significant differences, which include asking more and harder questions of high-expectancy students, being friendlier with high-expectancy students, and interacting more frequently with high-expectancy students.

The third strategy (using nonverbal and verbal indicators of respect) enacts equal and positive behavior toward reluctant students as quickly as possible. At this stage, such behaviors might be very general, like taking time to interact with reluctant students, making sure teachers smile at and show affection toward reluctant students, and using humor with reluctant students.

When the strategies in this element produce the desired effects, teachers will observe the following behaviors in students.

- Students say the teacher cares for all students.
- Students treat each other with respect.

Element 42: Asking In-Depth Questions of Reluctant Learners

One of the most common ways that teachers treat reluctant students differently is that they do not ask them questions that are as complex as the questions they ask other students. Teachers commonly do this out of a desire to avoid embarrassing students. That is, a teacher will ask a reluctant student an easier question than he or she would ask other students in an effort to increase the chances that the reluctant student will answer it correctly. Unfortunately, although well intended, such behavior communicates an implicit message to reluctant learners that they are not expected to do very well. To counteract this, teachers should employ specific strategies. The strategies for this element appear in table 10.2.

Table 10.2: Asking In-Depth Questions of Reluctant Learners

Strategy	Description
Question levels	The teacher asks questions that require students to analyze information, evaluate conclusions, or make inferences. These types of questions are more complex than questions that test recognition or recall of correct answers. The teacher ensures that he or she frequently asks reluctant learners complex questions, even if these students may need help or encouragement to respond.
Response opportunities	The teacher reinforces high expectations for all students by giving them equal response opportunities. No student has significantly more or fewer opportunities to answer a question than any other student.
Follow-up questioning	If a student is having trouble answering a question, the teacher restates the question, encourages collaboration, or gives hints and cues. The teacher can also let the student opt out temporarily.
Evidence and support for student answers	To reinforce high expectations for all students, the teacher requires similar levels of evidence and support for answers from every student. If a student makes a claim, the teacher asks him or her to provide grounds and backing for that claim, regardless of whether the student is a typically reluctant learner.
Encouragement	To encourage participation from all class members, the teacher attributes ideas and comments to those who offer them. The teacher also thanks each student who asks a question or provides an answer, even if the answer is incorrect.
Wait time	The teacher provides appropriate wait time after asking a question and appropriate pause time between student answers to allow all students adequate time to process information and formulate responses.
Response tracking	The teacher ensures that all students have equal opportunities to respond by calling on any student instead of only selecting those who raise their hands. The teacher also keeps track of which students have answered or been asked questions, perhaps by placing a checkmark on his or her class chart next to student names.
Inappropriate reactions	The teacher encourages reluctant learners to answer questions and share their thoughts by avoiding inappropriate reactions to student responses. The teacher avoids any of the following responses: telling students they should have known the answer to a question, ignoring a student's response, making subjective comments about incorrect answers, or allowing negative comments from other students.

Source: Adapted from Marzano Resources, 2016c.

Some of the strategies in table 10.2 provide opportunities for reluctant learners to respond in a manner that allows their answers to be somewhat anonymous. For example, the strategy of response opportunities includes techniques like on your own. Here, students write their answer to a teacher's question on a piece of paper and place the answer on their desk, easily readable by the teacher. The teacher checks student answers while walking around the classroom, making mental notes of those students who might require help.

Some strategies provide scaffolding for students' answers. For example, when using the strategy of follow-up questioning, the teacher provides students with multiple opportunities to respond to a question by:

- Restating a question if a student is having trouble answering
- Asking students to collaborate if a student is having trouble answering a question
- Giving a student hints or cues if he or she is having trouble answering a question
- Letting a student off the hook temporarily if he or she is having trouble answering

Some strategies provide encouragement to reluctant learners. For example, the strategy of encouragement includes techniques like:

- Acknowledging any correct portion of a student's response
- Explaining how to alter incorrect responses to make them correct
- Identifying the question for an incorrect response

When the strategies in this element produce the desired effects, teachers will observe the following behaviors in students.

- Students say the teacher expects everyone to participate.
- Students say the teacher asks difficult questions of everyone.

Element 43: Probing Incorrect Answers With Reluctant Learners

Probably the most powerful way to communicate high expectations for reluctant learners is to interact with them in a rigorous manner when they respond incorrectly to a question. Indeed, this is a common practice when a high-expectancy student answers a question incorrectly. The same deference should be paid to reluctant students. The strategies for this element appear in table 10.3.

Table 10.3: Probing Incorrect Answers With Reluctant Learners

Strategy	Description
Using an appropriate response process	The teacher responds appropriately to incorrect or incomplete responses by first demonstrating gratitude for the student's response. Next, the teacher points out what is correct and what is incorrect about the student's response.
Letting students off the hook temporarily	If a student becomes flustered, confused, or embarrassed while answering a question, the teacher lets the student pass temporarily. However, the teacher returns to the same student at a later time (in either a whole-class or one-on-one context) and asks him or her to answer a different question or think through the initial question when the student feels calmer.
Using answer revision	The teacher uses elaborative interrogation techniques to help a student realize his or her answer is indefensible. The teacher responds to a student's incorrect answer with questions such as, "How do you know that to be true?" and "What evidence can you give to support that conclusion?"
Using think-pair-share	The teacher uses this structure to allow reluctant learners time to rehearse and correct answers before sharing them in front of the class. After a question, the teacher has students form pairs and tell their partners their best answers to the question. After two to three minutes of discussion in pairs, the teacher calls on a student. When called on, students can provide their own answer to the question, quote their partner's answer, or ask their partner to give his or her answer.

Source: Adapted from Marzano Resources, 2016aa.

All of the strategies in table 10.3 query students when they answer incorrectly in a manner that honors their responses but probes their thinking. Teachers tend to use these strategies in an integrated fashion. For example, a teacher might begin an interaction with a reluctant student who has answered incorrectly by thanking him for the answer. The teacher could next acknowledge the parts of the answer that were correct. The teacher would then help the student correct the errors by restating the question in such a way that provides a pathway to correction or reminds the student of class content that would correct the answer. If the situation warrants it, the teacher might let the student off the hook by providing time for the student to think about the answer and then coming back to the student for a revised response. During this interval, the teacher asks related questions of high-expectancy students to provide some hints and scaffolding for the reluctant student.

When the strategies in this element produce the desired effects, teachers will observe the following behaviors in students.

- Students say the teacher won't let them off the hook.
- Students say the teacher won't give up on them.
- Students say the teacher helps them think deeply about the content.
- Students say the teacher helps them answer difficult questions successfully.

Planning

The design question for communicating high expectations is, What strategies will I use to help typically reluctant students feel valued and comfortable interacting with me or their peers? The three elements that pertain to this design area provide specific guidance regarding this overall design question. Teachers can easily turn these elements into more focused planning questions.

- **Element 41:** How will I communicate value and respect for reluctant learners?
- **Element 42:** How will I ensure that I ask in-depth questions of reluctant learners?
- **Element 43:** How will I probe incorrect answers with reluctant learners?

When planning for this design question, the teacher must begin by thinking of those students whom he or she is not pushing to excel. Planning to communicate high expectations, by definition, means focusing on those students for whom the teacher and others have—wittingly or unwittingly—communicated low expectations. This type of planning, then, might lead the teacher to identify and examine his or her biases and the manner in which he or she treats students differently. This provides the basis to ensure that all students are challenged and treated in a way that communicates high expectations. On a daily basis, the teacher plans and engages in explicit behaviors to ensure that reluctant learners receive the message that their thinking is valued and they are expected to perform at high levels.

Implications for Change

The major change this design area implies involves enhanced awareness on the teachers' part regarding their expectations for students and the possible negative consequences. Specifically, communicating high expectations for all students means that teachers must be aware of the fact that they have different expectations and thus engage in differential treatment of students.

The implications for this design area are obviously related to the implications for the design area of relationships. Both deal with enhanced teacher awareness regarding the manner in which they think and its effect on their actions. The book *Managing the Inner World of Teaching* (Marzano & Marzano, 2015) addresses this topic in depth. Briefly though, the first awareness that teachers should cultivate is the natural human process of categorization. Albert Einstein (1970) explains that "thinking without the positing of categories and of concepts in general would be as impossible as breathing in a vacuum" (p. 674). We form categories about people by what others tell us, particularly when we are young and impressionable. We also create categories based on our observations. Both of these processes can result in biases. One of the most important aspects of categories we form is that we have generalizations associated with each category. Charles G. Lord and Cheryl A. Taylor (2009) note, "People so readily generalize that they often 'know' in advance what they are going to 'like' and what they are going to 'dislike'" (p. 827). If a teacher's category for low-expectancy students includes generalizations like "these students simply won't try very hard" or "these students will give up if they are challenged," then he or she will act accordingly.

The second awareness teachers should cultivate is that we have scripts associated with our categories and their related generalizations. Marzano and Marzano (2015) explain that scripts are habitual ways of acting in specific situations. We have scripts for what we do in the morning after we get up. We have scripts for how we interact with new people we meet. Teachers have scripts for how they introduce new content, how they interact with high-expectancy students, and how they interact with low-expectancy students. It is this latter set of scripts that mutes the instruction to reluctant learners. Teachers' scripts for this category of students don't involve the engaging, challenging, and acknowledging behaviors that are inherent in scripts for high-expectancy students.

Teacher preservice and postservice preparation has traditionally focused on instructional strategies that do not require teachers to examine themselves, but I believe that teachers' self-awareness regarding categories and scripts is an untapped source of effective classroom strategies. The more teachers are aware of their own tendencies as human beings, the more they are aware of these same tendencies in students. Such awareness can only enhance teachers' ability to interact with students. One can also make the case that such awareness will enhance teachers' lives outside of the classroom.

CHAPTER 11

Making System Changes

Teachers function within the context of at least two systems: (1) the school and (2) the district. Those systems enhance individual teachers' effectiveness and contribute to the ineffectiveness of individual teachers, usually simultaneously. While schools and districts certainly have policies that help classroom teachers, they also have policies (some long-standing) that are glaring impediments to effective teaching. These impediments can and should be addressed. Here I recommend eight system changes that naturally flow from the changes *The New Art and Science of Teaching* implies.

The recommendations in this chapter are based on the changes chapters 1 through 10 imply, but go well beyond them. Indeed, they even go beyond the confines of an instructional model like *The New Art and Science of Teaching*. They represent my personal beliefs about system changes that are essential if K–12 education is to rise to its next level of effectiveness. As the discussion in the introductory chapter indicates, they represent my manifesto on education.

Recommendation 1: Create a System That Ensures Teacher Development

The most obvious systems change *The New Art and Science of Teaching* implies is to systematically support teacher growth. I have discussed this in a number of publications (Marzano, 2012; Marzano et al., 2016; Marzano & Simms, 2013; Marzano & Toth, 2013). Briefly though, such a system involves a detailed analysis of each teacher's strengths and weaknesses in the forty-three elements of the model. To accomplish this, teachers would use a scale like that in figure 11.1 (page 104).

As its name implies, the developmental scale is designed for teacher development in the elements of *The New Art and Science of Teaching*. Teachers use the scale in figure 11.1 to examine his or her use of a specific strategy. At score 0 (not using), the teacher should be using the strategy but is not. At score 1 (beginning), the teacher is using the strategy but with errors or omissions. At score 2 (developing), the teacher is executing the strategy without error but not monitoring students to see if the strategy is having the desired effect. At score 3 (applying), the teacher is executing the strategy without error and monitoring its effect on students. Based on feedback from students, the teacher makes changes to ensure that at least the majority of students are reaping the desired effects from the strategy. At score 4 (innovating), the teacher makes enough adaptations that all students are experiencing the strategy's desired effects.

4 Innovating	I adapt behaviors and create new strategies for unique student needs and situations.
3 Applying	I use the strategies and behaviors associated with this element, and I monitor the extent to which my actions affect students.
2 Developing	I use the strategies and behaviors associated with this element, but I do not monitor the effect on students.
1 Beginning	I use the strategies and behaviors associated with this element incorrectly or with parts missing.
0 Not Using	I am unaware of strategies and behaviors associated with this element.

Figure 11.1: Developmental scale for elements.

Note that the scale in figure 11.1 is generic. Visit **go.SolutionTree.com/instruction** for samples and more information on scales specific to each of the forty-three elements in *The New Art and Science of Teaching*. To illustrate, figure 11.2 contains the scale specific to element 24 for increasing response rates.

4 Innovating	I adapt behaviors and create new strategies for unique student needs and situations.
3 Applying	I use response-rate techniques to maintain student engagement, and I monitor the extent to which the techniques keep students engaged.
2 Developing	I use response-rate techniques to maintain student engagement in questions, but I do not monitor the effect on students.
1 Beginning	I use the strategies and behaviors associated with this element incorrectly or with parts missing.
0 Not Using	I am unaware of strategies and behaviors associated with this element.

Source: Marzano Resources, 2016r.

Figure 11.2: Scale for response rates.

Note that the scale is written in the first person, from the teacher's perspective. This provides a perspective that focuses on self-development. I recommend five steps in the teacher development process.

1. Teachers start with a self-audit.
2. Teachers keep track of their progress.
3. Teachers have opportunities to observe and discuss effective teaching.
4. Teachers use collaborative teaming within the PLC process.
5. Teachers have opportunities to engage in coaching.

Start With a Self-Audit

Teacher development begins with a self-audit. In a number of publications, I describe the basic process of a self-audit (Marzano, 2012; Marzano, Frontier, & Livingston, 2011; Marzano & Toth, 2013). Briefly though, each year, teachers begin by rating themselves on the developmental scales for the forty-three elements in *The New Art and Science of Teaching* model. Based on the self-audit, they select one to three elements where they will focus their development over the year. These are typically elements for which they initially rate themselves as 0 (not using), 1 (beginning), or 2 (developing). Supervisors might verify teacher selections as appropriate choices for a given teacher. For each area, teachers set growth goals using the scale. At a minimum, growth goals should include reaching score 3 (applying) status by the end of the year.

Keep Track of Progress

After setting growth goals, teachers begin practicing the strategies they have selected. As they practice, they keep anecdotal records of their progress, like those depicted in figure 11.3.

9/12	I used a free-flowing web to introduce the writing process. It was not very effective at first because I explained how the web works instead of showing students how to use it. The class seemed to like the exercise, though, so I would like to keep trying to use the webs.
9/21	Today we used free-flowing webs to brainstorm ideas for an essay. Once my students had selected topics for their essays, they mapped out main ideas and details using another web. It worked well, but the circles tended to get disorganized.
10/5	Today I tried asking students to use free-flowing webs to compare two things, and it worked really well. They drew the two things they were comparing in two big circles on the left and right of a page and wrote descriptors and facts in smaller circles around them. Then they connected the big circles to all the descriptors and facts that applied to them. There were some really interesting webs that helped the students see connections they hadn't realized before.
10/14	Today the counselor came in to do a career lesson, and I asked her to use a free-flowing web as a part of her lesson, because the students were already familiar with it. They really caught on to the idea of putting themselves in the center circle and then filling in their life goals in the surrounding circles. Some of them even made circles to show what they would have to do to achieve their goals.
10/20	Now that my students are comfortable with free-flowing webs, we've started using them to show relationships, and a few of my students even adapted the web for use with pictures. Almost like a storyboard, they planned out narrative pieces by drawing different events from their stories, and then found connections between the events and characters by drawing lines.

Source: Marzano, 2012.

Figure 11.3: Teacher anecdotal records.

The anecdotal records in figure 11.3 deal with a specific knowledge representation strategy referred to as the *free-flowing web* (see table 3.3 in element 8, page 32). Teachers also keep track of their progress on the developmental scale as depicted in figure 11.4 (page 106).

Observe and Discuss Effective Teaching

It stands to reason that teachers need to observe other teachers and discuss the intricacies of teaching if they are to improve. As the book *Collaborative Teams That Transform Schools* (Marzano et al., 2016) describes, instructional rounds involve teachers observing other teachers. Observations are not made to evaluate or critique other teachers. Rather, teachers observe other teachers to learn from them. Consequently, the observed teachers are typically the best teachers in a building so that they might provide positive examples of strategy use. At the end of one or more observations, observing teachers meet to caucus and discuss the strategies they witnessed being used and what they learned from the experience. Teachers should have the opportunity to participate in instructional rounds at least twice per year.

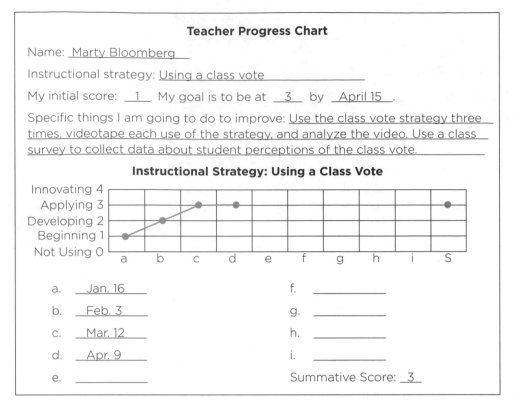

Source: Marzano, 2012.

Figure 11.4: Teacher tracking chart.

Use Collaborative Teaming Within the PLC Process

The PLC process is one of the most popular innovations in the United States. Marzano and colleagues (2016) describe this process, developed by Richard DuFour, Rebecca DuFour, and Robert Eaker (DuFour et al., 2016), as "all the policies and practices that lead a school to establish and maintain a network of collaborative teams whose work enhances the learning of students" (p. 17). A collaborative team is a group of teachers "working together to improve student learning" (DuFour et al., 2016, p. 17).

In the past, the primary purpose of collaborative teams has been to design common formative assessments, administer and score them, and then interpret them in terms of students' strengths and weaknesses. While this is a powerful activity, collaborative teams can also help team members develop their skill in specific instructional strategies. That is, collaborative teams might form around strategies selected for development. For example, those teachers who have set goals for improvement of response rate strategies would form a team, as would those teachers who set developmental goals for motivating and inspiring students, and so on. These collaborative teams might last only a month or so during which time team members share experiences with selected strategies and even visit each other's classes.

Engage in Coaching

As Marzano and Toth (2013) describe, coaching is critical to helping teachers advance in their pedagogical skills. The developmental scales are designed for coaching. For example, once a teacher has identified his or her skill level on the developmental scale, it is fairly straightforward to coach teachers to the next level. This is depicted in figure 11.5.

4 Innovating	The coach helps the teacher adapt strategies or create new strategies that meet the needs of students for whom the typical use of the strategy does not work.
3 Applying	The coach helps the teacher understand the desired effect on students for the strategy and helps the teacher develop strategies to monitor whether the strategy is having the desired effect in the classroom.
2 Developing	The coach helps the teacher eliminate errors in the use of the strategy.
1 Beginning	The coach helps the teacher understand or develop the steps in the strategy. The coach facilitates the teacher's initial trials of the strategy.
0 Not Using	The coach explains why the strategy is important and provides a general sense of the strategy.

Source: Adapted from Marzano & Toth, 2013.

Figure 11.5: Coaching behaviors associated with each level of the developmental scale.

As shown in figure 11.5, if a teacher is at level 0 (not using), the coach explains why the strategy is important and helps that teacher develop a general understanding of the strategy. This moves the teacher to the beginning level (1). To help the teacher move to the developing level (2), the coach helps the teacher identify his or her errors or omissions in the use of the strategy, and so on.

Recommendation 2: Focus on Unit Planning as Opposed to Lesson Planning

Perhaps the easiest change *The New Art and Science of Teaching* implies deals with planning. Across the United States, the vast majority of teachers must design and oftentimes turn in lesson plans for each subject area each day. The problem with this practice is that daily lesson planning is oftentimes simply a bureaucratic ritual with which teachers comply. Indeed, the concept of a lesson plan makes little sense since a teacher executes a lesson within the context of a set of lessons, oftentimes referred to as a *unit*, that serve a common purpose. As described in previous chapters, these lessons can take at least three distinct forms: (1) direct instruction, (2) practicing and deepening, and (3) knowledge application. In fact, two or more of these lesson types frequently appear in a single class period.

I believe it is an ineffective practice to plan one lesson at a time. Instead, teachers should plan from the perspective of the unit, which should provide an overarching framework for instruction. I like to refer to this initial plan as a *draft unit plan*. This name helps communicate the fact that a unit of instruction is always a work in progress.

In designing a draft unit plan, teachers should be free to adjust daily activities as the unit progresses to take advantage of learning opportunities that might come up or to revise activities based on student feedback. Although this implies a need for flexibility, it does not imply that units should not be well-thought-out. To walk this middle ground between flexibility and thoughtful design, I recommend a straightforward design such as the example in figure 11.6.

Day 1	Present and explain the proficiency scale for the unit (design question 1).
	Introduce the topic of central tendency using a Khan Academy video (design question 3).
	Provide direct instruction on key vocabulary terms (design question 3).
	Assign homework to read chapter in book (design question 6).

Figure 11.6: Sample draft unit plan on central tendency and dispersion.

continued →

Day 2	Brief review of content (design question 6).
	Watch Khan Academy clip depicting the concept of central tendency (design question 3).
	Model the procedures for computing mean, median, and mode (design question 4).
	Engage students in guided practice regarding computing mean, median, and mode (design question 4).
	Homework is to engage in independent practice regarding computing mean, median, and mode (design question 6).
Day 3	Remind students about learning goals and the proficiency scale (design question 1).
	Have students assess their current level of knowledge relative to the proficiency scale (design question 2).
	Do comparison activity involving the concepts of mean, median, and mode (design question 4).
Day 4	Test on mean, median, and mode (design question 2).
	Introduce concept of dispersion and measures of dispersion using Khan Academy clip (design question 3).
	Model the procedures for computing standard deviation, range, and quartiles (design question 4).
	Engage students in guided practice regarding computing standard deviation, range, and quartiles (design question 4).
	Homework is to engage in independent practice regarding computing standard deviation, range, and quartiles (design question 6).
Day 5	Remind students about the learning goals and proficiency scale (design question 1).
	Have students assess their current level of knowledge relative to the proficiency scale (design question 2).
	Do error-analysis activity involving typical mistakes made when computing standard deviation, range, and quartiles (design question 4).
Day 6	Test on standard deviation, range, and quartiles (design question 2).
	Organize students into groups for data-collection activity and provide resources (design question 5).
Day 7	Have student groups collect data that they will analyze into a distribution (design question 5).
Day 8	Have student groups compute various measures of central tendency and dispersion using data collected by the class and represent the distribution using two types of graphs (design question 5).
Day 9	Have individual students describe, in writing, the measures of central tendency and dispersion they computed in their groups and the graphs they used to depict the data; each student makes and defends claims regarding the relative utility of the measures of central tendency and dispersion he or she computed and the relative utility of the two types of graphs he or she used to display the data (design questions 2 and 5).
Day 10	Conduct a whole-class review of the students' claims and defense of their claims (design questions 2 and 6).

In figure 11.6, the activities for each day of the sample unit are coded within the following design areas.

- **Design area 1:** Activities that provide and communicate clear learning goals
- **Design area 2:** Assessment activities
- **Design area 3:** Direct instruction lessons
- **Design area 4:** Practicing and deepening lessons
- **Design area 5:** Knowledge application lessons
- **Design area 6:** Strategies used in all lessons

It is important to note that the goal of such coding is to facilitate understanding of this particular example. However, it is not an expectation that teachers would include such coding when designing a flexible draft plan for a unit.

The draft unit plan in figure 11.6 begins with the presentation of the proficiency scale on central tendency and some direct instruction on vocabulary and details, some presented using a Khan Academy video. The teacher moves to practicing and deepening activities. The teacher uses such activities regularly throughout the unit. The lesson ends with a knowledge application task for which students generate and support claims. Activities that help students continually integrate new knowledge with old knowledge and revise understanding occur throughout the ten-day unit.

As illustrated in figure 11.6, the first six design questions in *The New Art and Science of Teaching* carry the brunt of the weight when it comes to planning. The first six design questions appear in figure 11.7.

Design Question 1	How will I communicate clear learning goals that help students understand the progression of knowledge they are expected to master and where they are along that progression?
Design Question 2	How will I design and administer assessments that help students understand how their test scores and grades are related to their status on the progression of knowledge they are expected to master?
Design Question 3	When content is new, how will I design and deliver direct instruction lessons that help students understand which parts are important and how the parts fit together?
Design Question 4	After presenting content, how will I design and deliver lessons that help students deepen their understanding and develop fluency in skills and processes?
Design Question 5	After presenting content, how will I design and deliver lessons that help students generate and defend claims through knowledge application?
Design Question 6	Throughout all types of lessons, what strategies will I use to help students continually integrate new knowledge with old knowledge and revise their understanding accordingly?

Figure 11.7: First six design questions.

These six questions are the heart of unit design. Teachers' thoughtful answers to these questions help ensure that students will progress through a well-articulated continuum of knowledge that is integrated with the knowledge addressed in other units.

Design questions 7 through 10 deal with the mental context for learning. Instead of building these into an overall unit plan, teachers should remind themselves of strategies in these areas on a daily basis. Teachers might use the form in figure 11.8 to this end. I refer to it as a *daily reminder* as opposed to a *daily lesson plan*.

What will I do to engage students today?

We'll play a vocabulary game.

What specific students must I pay attention to today and what actions will I take?

Maria and Brandon

- *Remind them about rules and procedures or acknowledge them.*

- *Go out of my way to establish positive relationships.*
  I'll engage Maria in a conversation.

- *Go out of my way to interact with reluctant learners.*
  I'll make sure I ask Brandon some difficult questions and stay with him if he has trouble with the answers.

Figure 11.8: Daily reminder form.

The first part of the daily reminder form deals specifically with engagement. This addresses design question 7. As discussed in chapter 7, engagement is the gateway to learning and represents a variety of mental states and processes, such as attention, energy, intrigue, and inspiration. Teachers should consider strategies to this end on a daily basis, making simple notes to remind them of activities that will most likely move students to high levels of engagement.

The second part of the daily reminder deals with design questions 8, 9, and 10—rules and procedures, relationships, and high expectations, respectively. Teachers should consider these on a daily basis as well simply because they represent such dynamic processes with circumstances and students' needs changing from day to day. Note that the second part of the daily reminder asks teachers to keep specific students in mind who might require special attention because they have greater needs than other students, or because the teacher habitually doesn't afford these students the same level of attention given to other students. The four design questions that relate to context appear in figure 11.9.

Design Question 7	What engagement strategies will I use to help students pay attention, be energized, be intrigued, and be inspired?
Design Question 8	What strategies will I use to help students understand and follow rules and procedures?
Design Question 9	What strategies will I use to help students feel welcome, accepted, and valued?
Design Question 10	What strategies will I use to help typically reluctant students feel valued and comfortable interacting with me or their peers?

Figure 11.9: Design questions for context.

Recommendation 3: Use Blended Instruction

With the advent of free Internet-based materials like Khan Academy (www.khanacademy.org), WolframAlpha (www.wolframalpha.com), and the like, blended learning is no longer the future of classroom instruction, it is the present. In *The New Art and Science of Teaching*, teachers should design Internet-based materials directly from proficiency scales. To illustrate, consider the proficiency scale in figure 11.10, which depicts the content for scores 2.0, 3.0, and 4.0.

4.0	Describe and defend what might occur to climatic patterns in a specific location given a dramatic change in one specific process of the water cycle.	• Descriptions of specific requirements of what student must address • Examples from previous students
3.0	Obtain an understanding of: • How the water cycle processes (condensation, precipitation, surface run-off, percolation, and evaporation) impact climate changes • The effects of temperature and pressure in different layers of Earth's atmosphere	• Khan Academy video • Teacher-created screencasts • Pages in a book • Practice sheets • Short formative assessments
2.0	Recognize and recall basic terms such as *climatic patterns*, *atmospheric layers*, *stratosphere*, and *troposphere*. Recognize or recall isolated details such as: • Precipitation is one of the processes of the water cycle. • The troposphere is one of the lowest portions of the Earth's atmosphere.	• Khan Academy video • Teacher-created screencasts • Pages in a book • Practice sheets • Short formative assessments

Figure 11.10: Proficiency scale with resources.

The right-hand column in figure 11.10 lists the Internet-based resources that might be made available to students. Some of these resources are from sites like Khan Academy. Some resources are teacher created using free screencast websites. Some resources are hardcopy directions, practice sheets, assessments, and even pages from books that have been turned into PDFs and stored electronically. Over time, the resources for each level of each scale expand, resulting in an electronic set of resources available to teacher and students alike on an anytime, anywhere basis.

Recommendation 4: Ensure a Guaranteed and Viable Curriculum Involving Cognitive and Metacognitive Skills

Chapter 1 focused on providing clear learning goals and objectives. It highlighted the use of proficiency scales as a strategy that focuses content into measurement topics articulated as clear progressions of knowledge. While the example in that chapter was about an individual teacher who organized the content by units of instruction, a schoolwide or districtwide effort can be transformative in nature. More specifically, I recommend that a district identify measurement topics, each accompanied by a proficiency scale, for each subject area and grade level.

One common mistake schools and districts make is trying to write a proficiency scale for each standard in their national, state, or local standards. The problem with this approach is that nsational, state, and local standards are far too numerous to teach in any given year. As described in chapter 1, the solution to this problem is for the school or (better yet) the district to identify a small set of essential topics at each grade level and subject area. Again, as mentioned in chapter 1, Julia Simms (2016) directs the development of such topics. In mathematics, English language arts, and science, Simms identifies a combined total of about five hundred topics, which averages about thirteen topics per grade level, per subject area across these three subject areas. This leaves ample room for the important sets of cognitive and metacognitive skills embedded in *The New Art and Science of Teaching*.

Cognitive skills are "those needed to effectively process information and complete tasks" (Marzano et al., 2013, p. 24). Cognitive skills are inherent in *The New Art and Science of Teaching* in the content design areas 3, 4, 5, and 6. Table 11.1 contains a list of common cognitive skills.

Table 11.1: Cognitive Skills

Cognitive Skill	Definition
Generating conclusions	Combining information to create new ideas
Identifying common logical errors	Analyzing conclusions or arguments for validity or truth
Presenting and supporting claims	Using reasons and evidence to support new ideas
Navigating digital sources	Finding relevant information online or in electronic resources and assessing its credibility
Problem solving	Navigating obstacles and limiting conditions to achieve a goal
Decision making	Methodically selecting the best option from among several good alternatives
Experimenting	Generating explanations for events or phenomena and testing the accuracy of those explanations
Investigating	Identifying questions about a topic, event, or idea and discovering answers, solutions, or predictions
Identifying basic relationships between ideas	Understanding and recognizing how two ideas are connected by time, cause, addition, or contrast
Generating and manipulating mental images	Creating images, symbols, or imagined situations in one's mind and using them to test ideas and solutions

Metacognitive skills are those that allow us to exert executive control over the complex tasks in which we engage. *The New Art and Science of Teaching* includes metacognitive skills, again in the content design areas. Table 11.2 contains a list of metacognitive skills.

Table 11.2: Metacognitive Skills in *The New Art and Science of Teaching*

Metacognitive Skill	Definition
Planning for goals and making adjustments	Setting long- or short-term goals, making plans to accomplish those goals, and making adjustments to plans as needed
Staying focused when answers and solutions are not immediately apparent	When engaged in trying to solve a complex problem, recognizing frustration and re-engaging in the task
Pushing the limits of one's knowledge and skills	Setting or adjusting goals so that they require acquiring new knowledge or skills, rather than staying within one's comfort zone
Generating and pursuing one's own standards of excellence	When working toward creating a product, determining what the end result should look like and how success will be judged
Seeking incremental steps	Acquiring knowledge or skills in manageable chunks to avoid becoming overwhelmed, and examining each part's relationship to the whole
Seeking accuracy	Analyzing sources of information for reliability and verifying information by consulting multiple sources
Seeking clarity	When taking in new information, noticing one's own confusion and seeking to alleviate it
Resisting impulsivity	Noticing the desire to react or form a conclusion and pausing to revise that response or collect more information
Seeking cohesion and coherence	Monitoring the relationships between individual parts of a system and the relationships between the parts and the whole and making adjustments if they are instable or not producing the desired results

Source: Marzano et al., 2017.

The cognitive and metacognitive skills represent an explicit curriculum of their own that teachers should teach and reinforce throughout the various grade levels. Tables 11.3 and 11.4 contain a recommended listing of the scope and sequence of cognitive skills at the K–8 and high school levels, respectively.

Table 11.3: Scope and Sequence of Cognitive Skills for Grades K–8

Cognitive Skill	K	1	2	3	4	5	6	7	8
Generating conclusions		X		X		X		X	
Identifying common logical errors			X		X		X		X
Presenting and supporting claims			X		X		X		X
Navigating digital sources							X	X	X
Problem solving		X		X		X	X	X	
Decision making			X		X		X		X
Experimenting		X			X	X		X	
Investigating				X	X		X		X
Identifying basic relationships between ideas	X	X	X	X					
Generating and manipulating mental images	X	X	X	X					

Source: Marzano et al., in press.

Table 11.4: Scope and Sequence of Cognitive Skills for High School

Cognitive Skill	9 English	9 Mathematics	9 Social Studies	9 Science	10 English	10 Mathematics	10 Social Studies	10 Science
Generating conclusions	X				X			
Identifying common logical errors	X				X			
Presenting and supporting claims	X			X	X			X
Navigating digital sources								
Problem solving		X				X		
Decision making			X				X	
Experimenting				X				X
Investigating	X		X		X		X	
Identifying basic relationships between ideas								
Generating and manipulating mental images								

Source: Marzano et al., in press.

As shown in table 11.3, teachers can reasonably distribute the cognitive skills throughout the K–8 curriculum. The early grade levels emphasize identifying basic relationships between ideas and generating and manipulating mental images because they are so basic to analyzing and processing information. Generating conclusions is emphasized throughout the K–8 spectrum. Presenting and supporting claims and its related skill of identifying common logical errors begins at grade 2 and continues on up. Navigating digital sources starts seriously at grade 5.

As indicated in table 11.4, the secondary level addresses cognitive skills somewhat differently, in that some fit well within specific subject areas. For example, presenting and supporting claims fits well with English language arts and science. Problem solving fits well within mathematics, experimenting with science, and investigating with English language arts and social studies. Finally, note that the cognitive skills are not taught explicitly after grade 10. By grade 11, students should understand and be able to execute these processes well enough that teachers can use them in any subject area at grades 11 and 12.

The metacognitive skills exhibit patterns similar to the cognitive skills. Table 11.5 (page 114) depicts the scope and sequence of metacognitive skills at the K–8 levels; table 11.6 (page 114) depicts the scope and sequence at the high school level.

Table 11.5: Scope and Sequence of Metacognitive Skills for Grades K–8

Metacognitive Skill	K	1	2	3	4	5	6	7	8
Planning for goals and making adjustments		X	X		X		X		X
Staying focused when answers and solutions are not immediately apparent		X		X		X		X	
Pushing the limits of one's knowledge and skills						X		X	
Generating and pursuing one's own standards of excellence					X				X
Seeking incremental steps			X		X		X		X
Seeking accuracy		X		X		X		X	
Seeking clarity	X		X		X				
Resisting impulsivity	X			X				X	
Seeking cohesion and coherence			X		X		X		X

Source: Marzano et al., in press.

Table 11.6: Scope and Sequence of Metacognitive Skills for High School

Metacognitive Skill	9 English	9 Mathematics	9 Social Studies	9 Science	10 English	10 Mathematics	10 Social Studies	10 Science
Planning for goals and making adjustments			X				X	
Staying focused when answers and solutions are not immediately apparent		X				X		
Pushing the limits of one's knowledge and skills	X				X			
Generating and pursuing one's own standards of excellence	X				X			
Seeking incremental steps								
Seeking accuracy				X				X
Seeking clarity				X				X
Resisting impulsivity		X				X		
Seeking cohesion and coherence	X				X			

Source: Marzano et al., in press.

As indicated in table 11.5, teachers can include some metacognitive skills like planning for goals and making adjustments somewhat uniformly across the curriculum. Others, like generating and pursuing one's own standards of excellence are more appropriate at higher grade levels. As illustrated in table 11.6, at the high school level, certain metacognitive skills seem to fit well with specific subject areas. For example, staying focused when answers and solutions are not immediately apparent fits well with mathematics, whereas seeking cohesion and coherence fits well with English language arts, particularly writing. Again, metacognitive skills are not directly taught after grade 10 since by then students should have developed enough skill with them to warrant their use in any subject area.

Recommendation 5: Rely on Classroom Measurement

Chapter 2 addressed assessment and introduced the concept of measurement as a replacement for the current emphasis on tests. As that chapter describes, this approach can be transformational for the classroom teacher. It can also be transformational for the school or district. Specifically, districts and schools can rely on classroom assessments to measure students' status and growth, as opposed to only using tests designed outside of the classroom. This latter perspective is the situation in which many schools and districts find themselves. They rely almost solely on benchmark assessments and end-of-course assessments as evidence that students have mastered essential content. This is not optimal for a number of reasons.

First, benchmark assessments and end-of-course assessments are not administered frequently enough to be useful for students and teachers. This is obvious with end-of-course assessments, since, by definition, they are administered only after instruction. While benchmark assessments are administered during the school year, they are commonly administered only intermittently (once per month or once per quarter). They are certainly more useful than end-of-course assessments, but don't meet the day-to-day feedback needs of teachers and students.

Second, the lack of frequency of benchmark assessments puts too much emphasis on individual tests. Any single assessment has a great deal of error that is a natural by-product of the fact that no assessment is a perfect measure of what a student knows or can do at a particular moment in time. Indeed, test designers provide metrics that tell us just how much confidence we can have in students' scores on a single assessment. One metric is the reliability coefficient, which ranges from 0.00 to 1.00. A test reliability of 0.00 means that the scores for students can't be trusted at all. If students were to retake the test over and over (and somehow magically forget that they had taken the test before), the students would receive completely different scores each time. Fortunately, companies that design end-of-course and benchmark assessments would never allow a test to be used if it had a reliability approaching zero. A test reliability of 1.00 means that educators can completely trust the score for students. If students were to retake the test over and over (again forgetting about previous administrations), they would always receive precisely the same scores. Unfortunately, companies that design end-of-course and benchmark assessments do not design tests with reliabilities of 1.00 simply because it's impossible.

The amount of error that is inherent in tests that have reliabilities less than 1.00 is depicted in table 11.7 (page 116).

Table 11.7: Ninty-Five Percent Confidence Intervals

Reliability	Observed Score	Lower Limit	Upper Limit	Range
0.85	75	69	81	12
0.75	75	67	83	16
0.65	75	65	85	20
0.55	75	64	86	22

Note: Standard deviation = 8.33.

Table 11.7 depicts the amount of trust (or lack thereof) one can have for individual scores on a single test. The score that a student receives on a test is the *observed score*. In this case, the observed score is the same in each situation: 75 points out of a possible 100 points. Since all observed scores include some error, a common convention is to compute what is referred to as the *95 percent confidence interval*—an interval of scores within which one is about 95 percent sure the student's true score actually falls. As indicated in table 11.7, the higher the reliability of a test, the smaller this interval. For example, assume that a student had an observed score of 75 on a test that had a reliability of 0.85. The interval in which one could be 95 percent certain that the true score probably falls would be 69 to 81. If the observed score of 75 occurred on a test that had a reliability of 0.55, the 95 percent confidence interval would be 64 to 86. Table 11.7 demonstrates graphically that a single score on any type of assessment is always an approximation of the score the student might truly deserve.

Third, the use of end-of-course and benchmark assessments as the primary information with which to measure students ignores the rich data that are available from classroom assessments. This is addressed in chapter 2, which dealt with assessments based on proficiency scales. Chapter 2 also introduced the concept of the measurement process as a new way of approaching classroom assessments. Briefly, all assessments should be designed using a specific proficiency scale so that they address the same content with well-defined levels. Through this, teachers track each student's scores over time so that each student's growth is readily observable.

One of the more powerful aspects of this type of tracking is that teachers can compute a very accurate estimation of each student's summative or final score. To illustrate, consider figure 11.11.

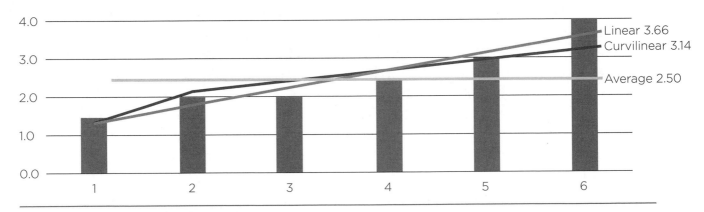

Figure 11.11: Mathematical models.

Figure 11.11 depicts one student's scores on six assessments for a particular proficiency scale. The student starts with an observed score of 1.50 and ends with an observed score of 4.00. Figure 11.11 also depicts three ways of computing a student's summative score, represented by the three lines through the student's observed scores. The straight horizontal line represents the average. If we used the average to summarize the student's scores, the summative score would be 2.50. The straight line increasing at equal intervals from left to right represents the linear trend in the student's scores. If we use this to estimate the student's summative score, the student would receive a score of 3.66. The curved line represents the curvilinear trend. If this were used to compute the student's summative score, the student would receive a score of 3.14. Each of these represent a mathematical estimate of the student's true status at the end of the grading period. Each approach assumes that observed scores contain error and each represents assumptions about student learning (Marzano, 2006; Marzano et al., in press).

The average operates on the assumption that no learning has occurred. Stated differently, the average is based on the assumption that the differences in the student's scores from assessment to assessment were simply due to error. If the student had received a perfectly accurate score on each assessment, all the scores would have been 2.50. The linear trend is based on the assumption that learning is best described by a gradual increase in scores from one assessment to another. Again, the model assumes that there was error in each assessment, but that the student's true status was always increasing with a final true score of 3.66. The curvilinear trend is based on the assumption that learning is best explained as rather large increases in scores at the beginning but then leveling off over time. If we accept this model, the student's final status would be predicted as 3.14.

There are mathematical formulas that evaluate which of the three models most closely follows the observed score (see Marzano, 2006; Marzano et al., in press). Additionally, there are Internet-based tools that automatically provide all computations for teachers. In the case of the patterns in figure 11.11, the linear trend best fits the data. Therefore, the most precise summative score to assign the student is 3.66.

Automated calculations like those shown in figure 11.11 allow schools and districts to compute precise scores for students that rely on teacher-designed assessments, thus altering the almost complete reliance on tests administered outside the confines of regular instruction.

Recommendation 6: Change Report Cards

The concepts of proficiency scales and measurement as presented in chapters 1 and 2 invite a re-examination of grades and report cards. In a series of works (Marzano, 2006, 2010b), I recommend a change in the report cards schools use to demonstrate students' status and growth. Such a report card appears in figure 11.12.

Name	Lori Fedorowicz
Address	1230 Grape Street
City	Anytown, CO 80000
Grade level	5

English Language Arts	2.56	B–		Generating Conclusions	2.70	B
Mathematics	3.18	A–		Navigating Digital Sources	3.50	A
Science	2.56	B–		Staying Focused	3.00	A–
Social Studies	2.94	B+		Seeking Accuracy	3.00	A–
Art	2.75	B				

Figure 11.12: Standards-referenced report card.

continued →

		0.5	1.0	1.5	2.0	2.5	3.0	3.5	4.0
English Language Arts									
Decoding	2.5								
Analyzing text organization and structure	1.5								
Analyzing ideas and themes	2.0								
Analyzing claims	3.5								
Analyzing narratives	2.5								
Comparing texts	1.0								
Analyzing words	2.5								
Generating text organization and structure	3.0								
Generating sentence structure	3.0								
Generating claims	3.0								
Using citations	2.5								
Generating narratives	2.5								
Generating point of view and purpose	3.0								
Writing for a specific audience	3.0								
Using specific words and parts of speech	3.0								
Using punctuation, capitalization, and spelling properly	2.0								
Engaging in revision and editing	3.0								
Average for English Language Arts	2.56								
Cognitive Skills (English Language Arts)									
Generating conclusions	2.5								
Navigating digital sources	3.5								
Metacognitive Skills (English Language Arts)									
Staying focused	3.0								
Seeking accuracy	3.0								
Mathematics									
Decimals	3.0								
Fractions	3.0								
Area	3.0								
Volume	2.5								
Multiplication	3.5								
Division	3.5								
Comparison symbols	4.0								
Exponents	3.0								
Ordered pairs and coordinate systems	3.0								
Addition and subtraction	4.0								
Perimeter	4.0								
Data representation	3.0								
Central tendency in data sets	3.0								
Numerical patterns	3.0								
Probability	3.0								

Symmetry	3.0									
Two-dimensional figures	4.0									
Basic functions	2.5									
Factors and multiples	2.5									
Measurement	3.0									
Average for Mathematics	3.18									
Cognitive Skills (Mathematics)										
Generating conclusions	3.0									
Navigating digital sources	3.5									
Metacognitive Skills (Mathematics)										
Staying focused	3.5									
Seeking accuracy	3.5									
Science										
Matter and its interactions	2.5									
Motion and stability: Forces and interactions	3.0									
Energy	3.0									
From molecules to organisms: Structures and processes	2.5									
Ecosystems: Interactions, energy, and dynamics	2.0									
Earth's place in the universe	2.0									
Earth's systems	2.0									
Earth and human activity	3.0									
Engineering design	3.0									
Average for Science	2.56									
Cognitive Skills (Science)										
Generating conclusions	2.5									
Navigating digital sources	3.5									
Metacognitive Skills (Science)										
Staying focused	2.5									
Seeking accuracy	2.5									
Social Studies										
History: Analyze and interpret historical sources	3.5									
History: Historical eras, individuals, groups, ideas and themes in regions of the Western Hemisphere	3.5									
Geography: Use geographic tools	3.0									
Geography: Human and physical systems	3.0									
Economics: Different economic systems	2.5									
Economics: Personal financial literacy	3.0									
Civics: Connection of the United States to other nations	2.5									

continued →

Civics: Multiple systems of government	2.5									
Average for Social Studies	2.94									
Cognitive Skills (Social Studies)										
Generating conclusions	3.0									
Navigating digital sources	3.5									
Metacognitive Skills (Social Studies)										
Staying focused	3.0									
Seeking accuracy	3.0									
Art										
Perceptual skills and visual arts vocabulary	3.0									
Art elements and principles of design	3.0									
Skills, processes, materials, and tools	2.5									
Communication and expression through original works of art	2.5									
Average for Art	2.75									
Cognitive Skills (Art)										
Generating conclusions	2.5									
Navigating digital sources	3.5									
Metacognitive Skills (Art)										
Staying focused	3.0									
Seeking accuracy	3.0									

█ = Student's first score at the beginning of the year.

▒ = Student's score on a proficiency scale at the end of the grading period.

Source: Adapted from Marzano et al., in press.

The bar graphs in figure 11.12 represent students' scores on specific proficiency scales. The dark part of each bar graph indicates a student's first score at the beginning of the year. The light part of each bar graph represents the student's score on a proficiency scale at the end of the grading period. As discussed in recommendation 5, teachers can compute students' final scores using mathematical models that best fit the data. For reporting purposes, these scores were rounded up or down to the nearest half-point or quarter-point score. I have found this to be a common practice in schools for ease of understanding.

The overall score for a subject area in the report card is computed by averaging the final scores on proficiency scale topics. To illustrate, consider English language arts. The proficiency scales addressed in this subject area are decoding; analyzing text organization and structure; analyzing ideas and themes; analyzing claims; analyzing narratives; comparing texts; analyzing words; generating text organization and structure; generating sentence structure; generating claims; using citations; generating narratives; generating point of view and purpose; writing for a specific audience; using specific words and parts of speech; using punctuation, capitalization, and spelling properly; and engaging in revision and editing. The teacher averaged the summative scores for these measurement topics to obtain the aggregate score of 2.56.

Also note that the report in figure 11.12 contains proficiency scale scores for cognitive and metacognitive skills. Specifically, each subject area reports scores for the following cognitive skills: generating conclusions and navigating digital sources. Each subject area reports scores for the following metacognitive skills: staying focused and seeking accuracy.

At the top of this report card are traditional letter grades. These are computed by translating the aggregate summative score into an overall grade using table 11.8.

There is a sound logic to the conversion scale in table 11.8. Since a score of 3.0 on a proficiency scale represents proficiency on the content, an average of 3.0 or above puts a student in the A category. An average score of 2.50 to 2.99 puts a student in the B category. A score of 2.5 indicates that across the topics the student knew the simpler content and had partial knowledge of the target content.

Table 11.8: Conversion from Proficiency Scale Scores to Letter Grades

Average Proficiency Scale Score	Letter Grade
3.75–4.00	A+
3.26–3.74	A
3.00–3.25	A–
2.84–2.99	B+
2.67–2.83	B
2.50–2.66	B–
2.34–2.49	C+
2.17–2.33	C
2.00–2.16	C–
1.76–1.99	D+
1.26–1.75	D
1.00–1.25	D–
Below 1.00	F

Source: Adapted from Marzano, 2010b.

Recommendation 7: Adjust Scheduling to Address the Differential Effectiveness of Teachers

Scheduling can be one of the most limiting practices in K–12 education. Traditional scheduling practices are grounded in the assumption that the same teacher will be with a specific group of students for an entire year for a given class period. This exacerbates the differential effects teachers have on students. To illustrate, assume that an elementary school has three teachers for each grade level. One teacher is highly competent, another teacher is moderately competent, and the third is not competent. All three teachers are teaching groups of students of precisely equal ability. As one might expect, the students in the class with the teacher who is highly competent will outperform the students in the class with the moderately competent teacher, whose students will outperform the students with the incompetent teacher. Researchers make this point in more concrete statistical terms. For example, as a result of the more tightly controlled studies of the differential effect of teachers, Barbara Nye, Spyros Konstantopoulos, and Larry B. Hedges (2004) conclude:

> These findings would suggest that the difference in achievement gains between having a 25th percentile teacher (a not so effective teacher) and a 75th percentile teacher (an effective teacher) is over one third of a standard deviation (0.35) in reading and almost

> half a standard deviation (0.48) in mathematics. Similarly, the difference in achievement gains between having a 50th percentile teacher (an average teacher) and a 90th percentile teacher (a very effective teacher) is about one third of a standard deviation (0.33) in reading and somewhat smaller than half a standard deviation (0.46) in mathematics. . . . These effects are certainly large enough effects to have policy significance. (p. 253)

In effect, the differential expertise of teachers in a building produces differential learning in students. Of course, one obvious solution is to ensure that all teachers are highly effective. While this should always be a goal, it is not readily attainable, particularly when one considers what is known about expertise. Specifically, developing expertise in a complex field like teaching requires about a decade of deliberate practice to accomplish (see Ericsson & Charness, 1994; Ericsson, Krampe, & Tesch-Romer, 1993). Clearly, few schools are going to easily attain the lofty goal of having all their teachers be highly effective, particularly schools that have a great deal of teacher turnover or a great many beginning teachers. While working toward the goal of enhancing the effectiveness of all teachers, there are at least three things schools can do.

The first is to increase the number of opportunities students have to experience direct instruction from highly effective teachers. If scheduling practices and facilities will allow, all students can assemble in the auditorium or all-purpose room to receive direct instruction lessons from the highly effective teachers. Highly effective teachers can develop screencasts or video recordings on the important content for each proficiency scale, as recommendation 3 of this chapter describes.

A second way to address the differential effectiveness of teachers is to schedule in such a way that students in a given class experience instruction from a variety of teachers. Educators can achieve this using a grouping and regrouping protocol. Specifically, each week (or so) students are grouped by their current level of performance on a specific proficiency scale in a specific subject area. For example, at the fifth-grade level, the focus in a given week might be on the English language arts topic of writing for specific audiences. Based on the proficiency scale for the topic, all students in the fifth grade are organized into three groups: (1) those working on score 2.0 content, (2) those working on score 3.0 content, and (4) those working on score 4.0 content. During English language arts period, students go to the teacher or teachers designated for instruction at their particular level. Some schools refer to the period for which this type of grouping occurs as *FIT*, which stands for *focused instructional time*. In general, the most effective teachers work with students who are still at the score 2.0 level since they most likely require the most expertise instructionally.

A third way to address the differential effectiveness of teachers is somewhat similar to establishing a FIT period. However, rather than forcing students into groups based on their performance on a specific topic, students are free to work with any teacher in the school qualified in a specific subject area. A single class period is then set aside during which all students have access to any qualified teacher. Teacher-student interactions might involve extra instruction on a specific level of a specific topic, students being assessed and scored in a specific level of a specific topic, and general interactions regarding any academic topic.

Recommendation 8: Gradually Move to a Competency-Based System

The most profound system change *The New Art and Science of Teaching* implies is to move toward a competency-based system. While there are various descriptions of the nature of competency-based education (see Marzano et al., in press), all have at their core the fact that students do not move to a higher level of content (fifth-grade mathematics, for example) until they demonstrate competence at the lower level (fourth-grade mathematics). In addition, students are at liberty to move as quickly or slowly through the levels as necessary. Of course, this would require changes in scheduling that are beyond the scope of this text (for a discussion, see Marzano et al., in press). Along with these issues, teachers must take a different perspective on instruction. Specifically, the differences between instruction in a traditional classroom and a competency-based classroom are most salient across four different organizational structures: (1) whole-class instruction, (2) small-group instruction, (3) individual instruction, and (4) peer-to-peer instruction.

Whole-Class Instruction

In a traditional system, whole-class instruction is the dominant activity. In a competency-based education system, its role is greatly diminished because at any point in time, students are working on different measurement topics. In a traditional classroom, the teacher presents every new topic to the entire class at the same time. In a competency-based education classroom, teachers introduce different topics to different students at different times. This is not to say that whole-class instruction is not a valuable tool in a competency-based classroom. Indeed, as the teacher senses that a majority of students are having difficulty with a common topic, the teacher plans short whole-class lessons to address these issues. Those students who are not having difficulty with the identified topic serve as resources for those having the most difficulty.

Small-Group Instruction

In a traditional classroom, small-group instruction occurs when a teacher observes an opportunity to differentiate instruction to focus on the needs of a small group of students. For example, a teacher might note that a few students are having difficulty with a particular level of content on the unit's proficiency scale. The teacher then sets aside instructional time to bring these students together and provide the necessary input and resources.

The same dynamic applies in a competency-based education classroom. However, in a competency-based education classroom, the teacher plans for small-group instruction on a daily basis. In fact, it is a dominant form of instruction.

Individual Instruction

Individual instruction, by definition, means that the teacher is working with individual students on a one-to-one basis. This usually occurs in a serendipitous fashion. As the teacher walks around the classroom and notices that a particular student is struggling, he or she gives individual attention to the student. In a competency-based classroom, the teacher plans for one-to-one instruction on a systematic basis. Each day the teacher identifies specific students who need individual attention on specific levels of specific scales.

Peer-to-Peer Instruction

In the traditional classroom, peer-to-peer instruction is quite rare. One reason for this is that it is difficult to match one student's strengths with another student's weaknesses. In a competency-based classroom, such matching is quite straightforward. This is because students' current scores on proficiency scales are always available to the teacher. On a daily basis, then, the teacher can match a student who has not demonstrated proficiency on a particular topic with a willing student who has. While students should never be forced to help others, a competency-based classroom that fosters this dynamic can create a powerful culture of collaboration and mutual support.

Table 11.9 summarizes the differences between instruction in a traditional system and a competency-based system across the four types of organizational structures.

Table 11.9: Comparison of Competency-Based Education and Traditional Instruction

Instructional Strategy	Traditional Instruction	Competency-Based Instruction
Whole-Class Instruction	• Is the predominant form or source of instruction for all content • Can involve direct instruction of new content, practicing and deepening, knowledge application, and general instructional strategies	• Happens only in specific situations, such as teaching cognitive and metacognitive skills, when the majority of students have a common problem, or for a specific measurement topic
Small-Group Instruction	• Occurs when groups of students have common problems	• Is a dominant mode of grouping • Is explicitly planned for on a daily basis
Individual Instruction	• Occurs to meet the needs of individual students as needed • Occurs serendipitously	• Occurs to meet the needs of individual students as needed • Is planned for regularly
Peer-to-Peer Instruction	• Rarely occurs	• Is a dominant form of instruction

Conclusion

The New Art and Science of Teaching is much more than a revision of the original *Art and Science of Teaching* (Marzano, 2007). While it has significant additions in terms of the number and types of strategies, the main shift is in perspective. Focus must be on students' mental states and processes, as opposed to teacher actions. This is not to say that teacher actions are unimportant. Indeed, it is teachers' actions that should create specific mental states and processes. Unfortunately, K–12 education seems to rarely get past examining what the teacher does. Consequently, *The New Art and Science of Teaching* identifies specific student indicators that reveal strategies are working for all of the forty-three elements in the model. *The New Art and Science of Teaching* also emphasizes the synergistic relationship between classroom assessment and feedback to teachers and students, along with a new view of the nature and purpose of classroom assessments. Finally, *The New Art and Science of Teaching* is my personal declaration or manifesto regarding eight changes in the policies of schools and districts that, when enacted, could transform the nature of K–12 schooling. I believe all of these changes are logical consequences of the implications of *The New Art and Science of Teaching* framework.

References and Resources

Achieve. (2013). *Next Generation Science Standards: DCI arrangements of the Next Generation Science Standards.* Washington, DC: Author. Accessed at www.nextgenscience.org/sites/default/files/NGSS%20DCI%20Combined%2011.6.13.pdf on July 12, 2016.

Alfieri, L., Brooks, P. J., Aldrich, N. J., & Tenenbaum, H. R. (2011). Does discovery-based instruction enhance learning? *Journal of Educational Psychology, 103*(1), 1–18.

Anderson, J. R. (1983). *The architecture of cognition.* Cambridge, MA: Harvard University Press.

Basileo, L. D., & Marzano, R. J. (2016, June 16–17). *The Marzano model: How much does it really matter?* Session presented at the Building Expertise Conference, Orlando, FL.

Basileo, L. D., Toth, M. A., & Kennedy, E. A. (2015, May). *Final report: Pinellas County Public Schools 2013–2014 multiple measures pilot results.* West Palm Beach, FL: Learning Sciences International.

Burns, M. K. (2004). Empirical analysis of drill ratio research: Refining the instructional level for drill tasks. *Remedial and Special Education, 25*(3), 167–173.

Cazden, C. B. (1986). Classroom discourse. In M. C. Wittrock (Ed.), *Handbook of research on teaching* (3rd ed., pp. 432–463). New York: Macmillan.

Chidester, T. R., & Grigsby, W. C. (1984). A meta-analysis of the goal setting performance literature. *Academy of Management Proceedings,* 202–206.

Conley, D. T. (2014). *Getting ready for college, careers, and Common Core: What every educator needs to know.* San Francisco: Jossey-Bass.

de Bono, E. (1998). *Six thinking hats* (rev. and updated ed.). Boston: Bay Back Books.

Donovan, J. J., & Radosevich, D. J. (1998). The moderating role of goal commitment on the goal difficulty–performance relationship: A meta-analytic review and critical reanalysis. *Journal of Applied Psychology, 83*(2), 308–315.

DuFour, R., DuFour, R., Eaker, R., Many, T. W., & Mattos, M. (2016). *Learning by doing: A handbook for Professional Learning Communities at Work.* Bloomington, IN: Solution Tree Press.

Dweck, C. S. (2006). *Mindset: The new psychology of success.* New York: Random House.

Einstein, A. (1970). Reply to criticisms. In P. A. Schilpp (Ed.), *Albert Einstein: Philosopher-scientist* (pp. 665–688). Evanston, IL: Library of Living Philosophers. (Original work published 1949)

Ericsson, K. A., & Charness, N. (1994). Expert performance: Its structure and acquisition. *American Psychologist, 49*(8), 725–747.

Ericsson, K. A., Krampe, R. T., & Tesch-Romer, C. (1993). The role of deliberate practice in the acquisition of expert performance. *Psychological Review, 100*(3), 363–406.

Fitts, P. M., & Posner, M. I. (1967). *Human performance.* Belmont, CA: Brooks/Cole.

Fuchs, L. S., & Fuchs, D. (1985). *The effect of measuring student progress toward long vs. short-term goals: A meta-analysis.* (ERIC Document Reproduction Service No. ED263142) Accessed at http://eric.ed.gov/?id=ED263142 on April 8, 2009.

Gollwitzer, P. M., & Sheeran, P. (2006). Implementation intentions and goal achievement: A meta-analysis of effects and processes. *Advances in Experimental Social Psychology, 38,* 69–119.

Graham, S., & Perin, D. (2007). *Writing next: Effective strategies to improve writing of adolescents in middle and high schools—A report to Carnegie Corporation of New York.* Washington, DC: Alliance for Excellent Education. Accessed at www.all4ed.org/publications/WritingNext/WritingNext.pdf on January 24, 2009.

Hattie, J. (1999, August 2). *Influences on student learning.* Inaugural professorial lecture given at the University of Auckland, New Zealand. Accessed at www.teacherstoolbox.co.uk/downloads/managers/Influencesonstudent.pdf on January 24, 2009.

Hattie, J. (2009). *Visible learning: A synthesis of over 800 meta-analyses relating to achievement.* New York: Routledge.

Hattie, J., & Timperley, H. (2007). The power of feedback. *Review of Educational Research, 77*(1), 81–112.

Haystead, M. W., & Marzano, R. J. (2009, August). *Meta-analytic synthesis of studies conducted at Marzano Research on instructional strategies.* Centennial, CO: Marzano Resources.

Heflebower, T., Hoegh, J. K., & Warrick, P. (2014). *A school leader's guide to standards-based grading.* Bloomington, IN: Marzano Resources.

Hunt, M. (1997). *How science takes stock: The story of meta-analysis.* New York: Russell Sage Foundation.

Klein, H. J., Wesson, M. J., Hollenbeck, J. R., & Alge, B. J. (1999). Goal commitment and the goal-setting process: Conceptual clarification and empirical synthesis. *Journal of Applied Psychology, 84*(6), 885–896.

Kluger, A. N., & DeNisi, A. (1996). The effects of feedback interventions on performance: A historical review, a meta-analysis, and a preliminary feedback intervention theory. *Psychological Bulletin, 119*(2), 254–284.

Kounin, J. S. (1970). *Discipline and group management in classrooms.* New York: Holt, Rinehart and Winston.

Kounin, J. S. (1983, November). *Classrooms: Individual or behavior settings? Monographs in teaching and learning* (General Series No. 1). Bloomington, IN: Indiana University, School of Education. (ERIC Document Reproduction Service No. ED240070)

Lipsey, M. W., & Wilson, D. B. (1993). The efficacy of psychological, educational, and behavioral treatment: Confirmation from meta-analysis. *American Psychologist, 48*(12), 1181–1209.

Locke, E. A., & Latham, G. P. (1990). *A theory of goal setting and task performance.* Englewood Cliffs, NJ: Prentice Hall.

Locke, E. A., & Latham, G. P. (2002). Building a practically useful theory of goal setting and task motivation: A 35-year odyssey. *American Psychologist, 57*(9), 705–717.

Lord, C. G., & Taylor, C. A. (2009). Biased assimilation: Effects of assumptions and expectations on the interpretation of new evidence. *Social and Personality Psychology Compass, 3*(5), 827–841.

Marzano, R. J. (1992). *A different kind of classroom: Teaching with dimensions of learning.* Alexandria, VA: Association for Supervision and Curriculum Development.

Marzano, R. J. (1998, December). *A theory-based meta-analysis of research on instruction.* Aurora, CO: Mid-continent Regional Educational Laboratory. (ERIC Document Reproduction Service No. ED427087)

Marzano, R. J. (2003a). *Classroom management that works: Research-based strategies for every teacher.* Alexandria, VA: Association for Supervision and Curriculum Development.

Marzano, R. J. (2003b). *What works in schools: Translating research into action.* Alexandria, VA: Association for Supervision and Curriculum Development.

Marzano, R. J. (2006). *Classroom assessment and grading that work*. Alexandria, VA: Association for Supervision and Curriculum Development.

Marzano, R. J. (2007). *The art and science of teaching: A comprehensive framework for effective instruction*. Alexandria, VA: Association for Supervision and Curriculum Development.

Marzano, R. J. (2009a). *Designing and teaching learning goals and objectives*. Bloomington, IN: Marzano Resources.

Marzano, R. J. (2009b). Setting the record straight on "high-yield" strategies. *Phi Delta Kappan, 91*(1), 30–37.

Marzano, R. J. (2010a). Developing expert teachers. In R. J. Marzano (Ed.), *On excellence in teaching* (pp. 213–245). Bloomington, IN: Solution Tree Press.

Marzano, R. J. (2010b). *Formative assessment and standards-based grading*. Bloomington, IN: Marzano Resources.

Marzano, R. J. (2011). The perils and promises of discovery learning. *Educational Leadership, 69*(1), 86–87.

Marzano, R. J. (2012). *Becoming a reflective teacher*. Bloomington, IN: Marzano Resources.

Marzano, R. J. (2017). *Research base for* The New Art and Science of Teaching. Centennial, CO: Marzano Resources.

Marzano, R. J., Brandt, R. S., Hughes, C. S., Jones, B. F., Presseisen, B. Z., Rankin, S. C., et al. (1988). *Dimensions of thinking: A framework for curriculum and instruction*. Alexandria, VA: Association for Supervision and Curriculum Development.

Marzano, R. J., Frontier, T., & Livingston, D. (2011). *Effective supervision: Supporting the art and science of teaching*. Alexandria, VA: Association for Supervision and Curriculum Development.

Marzano, R. J., Heflebower, T., Hoegh, J. K., Warrick, P., & Grift, G. (2016). *Collaborative teams that transform schools: The next step in PLCs*. Bloomington, IN: Marzano Resources.

Marzano, R. J., & Kendall, J. S. (1996). *A comprehensive guide to designing standards-based districts, schools, and classrooms*. Alexandria, VA: Association for Supervision and Curriculum Development.

Marzano, R. J., & Kendall, J. S. (2007). *The new taxonomy of educational objectives* (2nd ed.). Thousand Oaks, CA: Corwin Press.

Marzano, R. J., & Kendall, J. S. (2008). *Designing and assessing educational objectives: Applying the new taxonomy*. Thousand Oaks, CA: Corwin Press.

Marzano, R. J., & Marzano, J. S. (2015). *Managing the inner world of teaching: Emotions, interpretations, and actions*. Bloomington, IN: Marzano Resources.

Marzano, R. J., Norford, J., Finn, M., & Finn, D. (in press). *A handbook for personalized competency-based education*. Bloomington, IN: Marzano Resources.

Marzano, R. J., & Pickering, D. J. (2007a). The case for and against homework. *Educational Leadership, 64*(6), 74–79.

Marzano, R. J., & Pickering, D. J. (2007b). Errors and allegations about research on homework. *Phi Delta Kappan, 88*(7), 507–513.

Marzano, R. J., & Pickering, D. J. (2007c). *Response to Kohn's allegations*. Centennial, CO: Marzano and Associates.

Marzano, R. J., & Pickering, D. J. (2011). *The highly engaged classroom*. Bloomington, IN: Marzano Resources.

Marzano, R. J., Pickering, D. J., & Pollock, J. E. (2001). *Classroom instruction that works: Research-based strategies for increasing student achievement*. Alexandria, VA: Association for Supervision and Curriculum Development.

Marzano, R. J., Scott, D., Boogren, T., & Newcomb, M. L. (2017). *Motivating and inspiring students: Strategies to awaken the learner*. Bloomington, IN: Marzano Resources.

Marzano, R. J., & Simms, J. A. (2013). *Coaching classroom instruction*. Bloomington, IN: Marzano Resources.

Marzano, R. J., & Simms, J. A. (2014). *Questioning sequences in the classroom*. Bloomington, IN: Marzano Resources.

Marzano, R. J., & Toth, M. D. (2013). *Teacher evaluation that makes a difference: A new model for teacher growth and student achievement*. Alexandria, VA: Association for Supervision and Curriculum Development.

Marzano, R. J., Yanoski, D. C., Hoegh, J. K., & Simms, J. A. (2013). *Using Common Core standards to enhance classroom instruction and assessment.* Bloomington, IN: Marzano Resources.

Marzano Resources. (2010). *What works in Oklahoma schools: Phase I state report.* Centennial, CO: Author.

Marzano Resources. (2011). *What works in Oklahoma schools: Phase II state report.* Centennial, CO: Author.

Marzano Resources. (2016a). *Acknowledging adherence to rules and procedures.* Centennial, CO: Author.

Marzano Resources. (2016b). *Acknowledging lack of adherence to rules and procedures.* Centennial, CO: Author.

Marzano Resources. (2016c). *Asking in-depth questions of reluctant learners.* Centennial, CO: Author.

Marzano Resources. (2016d). *Celebrating success.* Centennial, CO: Author.

Marzano Resources. (2016e). *Chunking content.* Centennial, CO: Author.

Marzano Resources. (2016f). *Demonstrating intensity and enthusiasm.* Centennial, CO: Author.

Marzano Resources. (2016g). *Demonstrating value and respect for reluctant learners.* Centennial, CO: Author.

Marzano Resources. (2016h). *Demonstrating withitness.* Centennial, CO: Author.

Marzano Resources. (2016i). *Displaying objectivity and control.* Centennial, CO: Author.

Marzano Resources. (2016j). *Elaborating on information.* Centennial, CO: Author.

Marzano Resources. (2016k). *Engaging students in cognitively complex tasks.* Centennial, CO: Author.

Marzano Resources. (2016l). *Establishing rules and procedures.* Centennial, CO: Author.

Marzano Resources. (2016m). *Examining errors in reasoning.* Centennial, CO: Author.

Marzano Resources. (2016n). *Examining similarities and differences.* Centennial, CO: Author.

Marzano Resources. (2016o). *Formal assessments of individual students.* Centennial, CO: Author.

Marzano Resources. (2016p). *Generating and defending claims.* Centennial, CO: Author.

Marzano Resources. (2016q). *Highlighting critical information.* Centennial, CO: Author.

Marzano Resources. (2016r). *Increasing response rates.* Centennial, CO: Author.

Marzano Resources. (2016s). *Informal assessments of the whole class.* Centennial, CO: Author.

Marzano Resources. (2016t). *Maintaining a lively pace.* Centennial, CO: Author.

Marzano Resources. (2016u). *Motivating and inspiring students.* Centennial, CO: Author.

Marzano Resources. (2016v). *Noticing when students are not engaged and reacting.* Centennial, CO: Author.

Marzano Resources. (2016w). *Organizing students to interact.* Centennial, CO: Author.

Marzano Resources. (2016x). *Organizing the physical layout of the classroom.* Centennial, CO: Author.

Marzano Resources. (2016y). *Presenting unusual information.* Centennial, CO: Author.

Marzano Resources. (2016z). *Previewing.* Centennial, CO: Author.

Marzano Resources. (2016aa). *Probing incorrect answers with reluctant learners.* Centennial, CO: Author.

Marzano Resources. (2016bb). *Processing content.* Centennial, CO: Author.

Marzano Resources. (2016cc). *Providing opportunities for students to talk about themselves.* Centennial, CO: Author.

Marzano Resources. (2016dd). *Providing resources and guidance.* Centennial, CO: Author.

Marzano Resources. (2016ee). *Providing scales and rubrics.* Centennial, CO: Author.

Marzano Resources. (2016ff). *Purposeful homework.* Centennial, CO: Author.

Marzano Resources. (2016gg). *Recording and representing knowledge.* Centennial, CO: Author.

Marzano Resources. (2016hh). *Reflecting on learning.* Centennial, CO: Author.

Marzano Resources. (2016ii). *Reviewing content*. Centennial, CO: Author.

Marzano Resources. (2016jj). *Revising knowledge*. Centennial, CO: Author.

Marzano Resources. (2016kk). *Structured practice sessions*. Centennial, CO: Author.

Marzano Resources. (2016ll). *Tracking student progress*. Centennial, CO: Author.

Marzano Resources. (2016mm). *Understanding students' backgrounds and interests*. Centennial, CO: Author.

Marzano Resources. (2016nn). *Using academic games*. Centennial, CO: Author.

Marzano Resources. (2016oo). *Using friendly controversy*. Centennial, CO: Author.

Marzano Resources. (2016pp). *Using physical movement*. Centennial, CO: Author.

Marzano Resources. (2016qq). *Using verbal and nonverbal behaviors that indicate affection for students*. Centennial, CO: Author.

Mento, A. J., Steel, R. P., & Karren, R. J. (1987). A meta-analytic study of the effects of goal setting on task performance: 1966–1984. *Organizational Behavior and Human Decision Processes, 39*(1), 52–83.

National Governors Association Center for Best Practices & Council of Chief State School Officers. (2010a). *Common Core State Standards for English language arts and literacy in history/social studies, science, and technical subjects*. Washington, DC: Authors. Accessed at www.corestandards.org/assets/CCSSI_ELA%20Standards.pdf on July 12, 2016.

National Governors Association Center for Best Practices & Council of Chief State School Officers. (2010b). *Common Core State Standards for mathematics*. Washington, DC: Authors. Accessed at www.corestandards.org/assets/CCSSI_Math%20Standards.pdf on July 12, 2016.

NGSS Lead States. (2013). *Next Generation Science Standards: For states, by states*. Washington, DC: National Academies Press.

Nye, B., Konstantopoulos, S., & Hedges, L. V. (2004). How large are teacher effects? *Educational Evaluation and Policy Analysis, 26*(3), 237–257.

Piaget, J. (1971). *Genetic epistemology* (E. Duckworth, Trans.). New York: Norton.

Rosenthal, R. (1956). *An attempt at an experimental induction of the defense mechanism of projection*. (Doctoral dissertation). University of California at Los Angeles.

Rosenthal, R., & Jacobson, L. (1968). *Pygmalion in the classroom: Teacher expectation and pupils' intellectual development*. New York: Holt, Rinehart and Winston.

Rumelhart, D. E., & Norman, D. A. (1978). Accretion, tuning and restructuring: Three modes of learning. In J. W. Cotton & R. L. Klatzky (Eds.), *Semantic factors in cognition* (pp. 37–53). Hillsdale, NJ: Erlbaum.

Simms, J. A. (2016, August). *The critical concepts*. Centennial, CO: Marzano Resources. Accessed at www.MarzanoResources.com/educational-services/critical-concepts on October 6, 2016.

Toulmin, S. (1958). *The uses of argument*. Cambridge, England, United Kingdom: Cambridge University Press.

Tubbs, M. E. (1986). Goal setting: A meta-analytic examination of the empirical evidence. *Journal of Applied Psychology, 71*(3), 474–483.

Utman, C. H. (1997). Performance effects of motivational state: A meta-analysis. *Personality and Social Psychology Review, 1*(2), 170–182.

Walberg, H. J. (1999). Productive teaching. In H. C. Waxman & H. J. Walberg (Eds.), *New directions for teaching practice and research* (pp. 75–104). Berkeley, CA: McCutchan.

Wise, K. C., & Okey, J. R. (1983). A meta-analysis of the effects of various science teaching strategies on achievement. *Journal of Research in Science Teaching, 20*(5), 415–435.

Wood, R. E., Mento, A. J., & Locke, E. A. (1987). Task complexity as a moderator of goal effects: A meta-analysis. *Journal of Applied Psychology, 72*(3), 416–425.

Wright, P. M. (1990). Operationalization of goal difficulty as a moderator of the goal difficulty–performance relationship. *Journal of Applied Psychology, 75*(3), 227–234.

Index

Solution Tree

Solution Tree's mission is to advance the work of our authors. By working with the best researchers and educators worldwide, we strive to be the premier provider of innovative publishing, in-demand events, and inspired professional development designed to transform education to ensure that all students learn.

ASCD is a global nonprofit association dedicated to the whole child approach that supports educators, families, community members, and policy makers. We provide expert and innovative solutions to facilitate professional development through print and digital publishing, on-site learning services, and conferences and events that empower educators to support the success of each child.